Recruitment Process Outsourcing R
Complete Self-Assessment Guide

The guidance in this Self-Assessment is based on Recruitment Process Outsourcing RPO best practices and standards in business process architecture, design and quality management. The guidance is also based on the professional judgment of the individual collaborators listed in the Acknowledgments.

Notice of rights

Trademarks

Table of Contents

About The Art of Service   8
Acknowledgments   9
Included Resources - how to access   9

Your feedback is invaluable to us   11
Purpose of this Self-Assessment   11
How to use the Self-Assessment   12
Recruitment Process Outsourcing RPO
Scorecard Example   14

Recruitment Process Outsourcing RPO
Scorecard   15

BEGINNING OF THE
SELF-ASSESSMENT: 16
CRITERION #1: RECOGNIZE   17

CRITERION #2: DEFINE: 24

CRITERION #3: MEASURE: 36

CRITERION #4: ANALYZE: 49

CRITERION #5: IMPROVE: 58

CRITERION #6: CONTROL: 70

CRITERION #7: SUSTAIN: 81
Recruitment Process Outsourcing RPO and Managing
Projects, Criteria for Project Managers: 107
1.0 Initiating Process Group: Recruitment Process
Outsourcing RPO   108

1.1 Project Charter: Recruitment Process Outsourcing RPO
                                                          110

1.2 Stakeholder Register: Recruitment Process Outsourcing RPO   112

1.3 Stakeholder Analysis Matrix: Recruitment Process Outsourcing RPO   113

2.0 Planning Process Group: Recruitment Process Outsourcing RPO   115

2.1 Project Management Plan: Recruitment Process Outsourcing RPO   118

2.2 Scope Management Plan: Recruitment Process Outsourcing RPO   120

2.3 Requirements Management Plan: Recruitment Process Outsourcing RPO   123

2.4 Requirements Documentation: Recruitment Process Outsourcing RPO   125

2.5 Requirements Traceability Matrix: Recruitment Process Outsourcing RPO   127

2.6 Project Scope Statement: Recruitment Process Outsourcing RPO   129

2.7 Assumption and Constraint Log: Recruitment Process Outsourcing RPO   131

2.8 Work Breakdown Structure: Recruitment Process Outsourcing RPO   133

2.9 WBS Dictionary: Recruitment Process Outsourcing RPO   135

2.10 Schedule Management Plan: Recruitment Process Outsourcing RPO   138

2.11 Activity List: Recruitment Process Outsourcing RPO 140

2.12 Activity Attributes: Recruitment Process Outsourcing RPO   142

2.13 Milestone List: Recruitment Process Outsourcing RPO   144

2.14 Network Diagram: Recruitment Process Outsourcing RPO   146

2.15 Activity Resource Requirements: Recruitment Process Outsourcing RPO   148

2.16 Resource Breakdown Structure: Recruitment Process Outsourcing RPO   150

2.17 Activity Duration Estimates: Recruitment Process Outsourcing RPO   152

2.18 Duration Estimating Worksheet: Recruitment Process Outsourcing RPO   154

2.19 Project Schedule: Recruitment Process Outsourcing RPO   156

2.20 Cost Management Plan: Recruitment Process Outsourcing RPO   158

2.21 Activity Cost Estimates: Recruitment Process Outsourcing RPO   160

2.22 Cost Estimating Worksheet: Recruitment Process Outsourcing RPO   162

2.23 Cost Baseline: Recruitment Process Outsourcing RPO   164

2.24 Quality Management Plan: Recruitment Process Outsourcing RPO   166

2.25 Quality Metrics: Recruitment Process Outsourcing RPO   168

2.26 Process Improvement Plan: Recruitment Process Outsourcing RPO   170

2.27 Responsibility Assignment Matrix: Recruitment Process Outsourcing RPO   172

2.28 Roles and Responsibilities: Recruitment Process Outsourcing RPO   174

2.29 Human Resource Management Plan: Recruitment Process Outsourcing RPO   176

2.30 Communications Management Plan: Recruitment Process Outsourcing RPO   178

2.31 Risk Management Plan: Recruitment Process Outsourcing RPO   180

2.32 Risk Register: Recruitment Process Outsourcing RPO 182

2.33 Probability and Impact Assessment: Recruitment Process Outsourcing RPO   184

2.34 Probability and Impact Matrix: Recruitment Process Outsourcing RPO   186

2.35 Risk Data Sheet: Recruitment Process Outsourcing RPO   188

2.36 Procurement Management Plan: Recruitment Process Outsourcing RPO   190

2.37 Source Selection Criteria: Recruitment Process Outsourcing RPO   192

2.38 Stakeholder Management Plan: Recruitment Process Outsourcing RPO   194

2.39 Change Management Plan: Recruitment Process Outsourcing RPO   196

3.0 Executing Process Group: Recruitment Process Outsourcing RPO   198

3.1 Team Member Status Report: Recruitment Process Outsourcing RPO   200

3.2 Change Request: Recruitment Process Outsourcing RPO   202

3.3 Change Log: Recruitment Process Outsourcing RPO   204

3.4 Decision Log: Recruitment Process Outsourcing RPO 206

3.5 Quality Audit: Recruitment Process Outsourcing RPO 208

3.6 Team Directory: Recruitment Process Outsourcing RPO   211

3.7 Team Operating Agreement: Recruitment Process Outsourcing RPO   213

3.8 Team Performance Assessment: Recruitment Process Outsourcing RPO   215

3.9 Team Member Performance Assessment: Recruitment Process Outsourcing RPO   217

3.10 Issue Log: Recruitment Process Outsourcing RPO   219

4.0 Monitoring and Controlling Process Group: Recruitment Process Outsourcing RPO   221

4.1 Project Performance Report: Recruitment Process Outsourcing RPO   223

4.2 Variance Analysis: Recruitment Process Outsourcing RPO   225

4.3 Earned Value Status: Recruitment Process Outsourcing RPO   227

4.4 Risk Audit: Recruitment Process Outsourcing RPO   229

4.5 Contractor Status Report: Recruitment Process Outsourcing RPO   231

4.6 Formal Acceptance: Recruitment Process Outsourcing RPO   233

5.0 Closing Process Group: Recruitment Process Outsourcing RPO   235

5.1 Procurement Audit: Recruitment Process Outsourcing RPO   237

5.2 Contract Close-Out: Recruitment Process Outsourcing RPO   239

5.3 Project or Phase Close-Out: Recruitment Process Outsourcing RPO   241

5.4 Lessons Learned: Recruitment Process Outsourcing RPO
                                                                    243
Index   246

About The Art of Service

The Art of Service, Business Process Architects since 2000, is dedicated to helping stakeholders achieve excellence.

Defining, designing, creating, and implementing a process to solve a stakeholders challenge or meet an objective is the most valuable role... In EVERY group, company, organization and department.

Unless you're talking a one-time, single-use project, there should be a process. Whether that process is managed and implemented by humans, AI, or a combination of the two, it needs to be designed by someone with a complex enough perspective to ask the right questions.

Someone capable of asking the right questions and step back and say, 'What are we really trying to accomplish here? And is there a different way to look at it?'

With The Art of Service's Standard Requirements Self-Assessments, we empower people who can do just that — whether their title is marketer, entrepreneur, manager, salesperson, consultant, Business Process Manager, executive assistant, IT Manager, CIO etc... —they are the people who rule the future. They are people who watch the process as it happens, and ask the right questions to make the process work better.

Contact us when you need any support with this Self-Assessment and any help with templates, blue-prints and examples of standard documents you might need:

http://theartofservice.com
service@theartofservice.com

Acknowledgments

This checklist was developed under the auspices of The Art of Service, chaired by Gerardus Blokdyk.

Representatives from several client companies participated in the preparation of this Self-Assessment.

Our deepest gratitude goes out to Matt Champagne, Ph.D. Surveys Expert, for his invaluable help and advise in structuring the Self Assessment.

In addition, we are thankful for the design and printing services provided.

Included Resources - how to access

Included with your purchase of the book is the Recruitment Process Outsourcing RPO Self-Assessment Spreadsheet Dashboard which contains all questions and Self-Assessment areas and auto-generates insights, graphs, and project RACI planning - all with examples to get you started right away.

How? Simply send an email to
access@theartofservice.com
with this books' title in the subject to get the Recruitment Process Outsourcing RPO Self Assessment Tool right away.

You will receive the following contents with New and Updated specific criteria:
- The latest quick edition of the book in PDF
- The latest complete edition of the book in PDF, which criteria correspond to the criteria in...
- The Self-Assessment Excel Dashboard, and...
- Example pre-filled Self-Assessment Excel Dashboard to get familiar with results generation
- ...plus an extra, special, resource that helps you with project

managing.

INCLUDES LIFETIME SELF ASSESSMENT UPDATES

Every self assessment comes with Lifetime Updates and Lifetime Free Updated Books. Lifetime Updates is an industry-first feature which allows you to receive verified self assessment updates, ensuring you always have the most accurate information at your fingertips.

Get it now- you will be glad you did - do it now, before you forget.

Send an email to **access@theartofservice.com** with this books' title in the subject to get the Recruitment Process Outsourcing RPO Self Assessment Tool right away.

Your feedback is invaluable to us

If you recently bought this book, we would love to hear from you! You can do this by writing a review on amazon (or the online store where you purchased this book) about your last purchase! As part of our continual service improvement process, we love to hear real client experiences and feedback.

How does it work?
To post a review on Amazon, just log in to your account and click on the Create Your Own Review button (under Customer Reviews) of the relevant product page. You can find examples of product reviews in Amazon. If you purchased from another online store, simply follow their procedures.

What happens when I submit my review?
Once you have submitted your review, send us an email at review@theartofservice.com with the link to your review so we can properly thank you for your feedback.

Purpose of this Self-Assessment

This Self-Assessment has been developed to improve understanding of the requirements and elements of Recruitment Process Outsourcing RPO, based on best practices and standards in business process architecture, design and quality management.

It is designed to allow for a rapid Self-Assessment to determine how closely existing management practices and procedures correspond to the elements of the Self-Assessment.

The criteria of requirements and elements of Recruitment Process Outsourcing RPO have been rephrased in the format of a Self-Assessment questionnaire, with a seven-criterion scoring system, as explained in this document.

In this format, even with limited background knowledge of

Recruitment Process Outsourcing RPO, a manager can quickly review existing operations to determine how they measure up to the standards. This in turn can serve as the starting point of a 'gap analysis' to identify management tools or system elements that might usefully be implemented in the organization to help improve overall performance.

How to use the Self-Assessment

On the following pages are a series of questions to identify to what extent your Recruitment Process Outsourcing RPO initiative is complete in comparison to the requirements set in standards.

To facilitate answering the questions, there is a space in front of each question to enter a score on a scale of '1' to '5'.

1 Strongly Disagree

2 Disagree

3 Neutral

4 Agree

5 Strongly Agree

Read the question and rate it with the following in front of mind:

**'In my belief,
the answer to this question is clearly defined'.**

There are two ways in which you can choose to interpret this statement;
  1. how aware are you that the answer to the question is clearly defined
  2. for more in-depth analysis you can choose to gather

evidence and confirm the answer to the question. This obviously will take more time, most Self-Assessment users opt for the first way to interpret the question and dig deeper later on based on the outcome of the overall Self-Assessment.

A score of '1' would mean that the answer is not clear at all, where a '5' would mean the answer is crystal clear and defined. Leave emtpy when the question is not applicable or you don't want to answer it, you can skip it without affecting your score. Write your score in the space provided.

After you have responded to all the appropriate statements in each section, compute your average score for that section, using the formula provided, and round to the nearest tenth. Then transfer to the corresponding spoke in the Recruitment Process Outsourcing RPO Scorecard on the second next page of the Self-Assessment.

Your completed Recruitment Process Outsourcing RPO Scorecard will give you a clear presentation of which Recruitment Process Outsourcing RPO areas need attention.

Recruitment Process Outsourcing RPO Scorecard Example

Example of how the finalized Scorecard can look like:

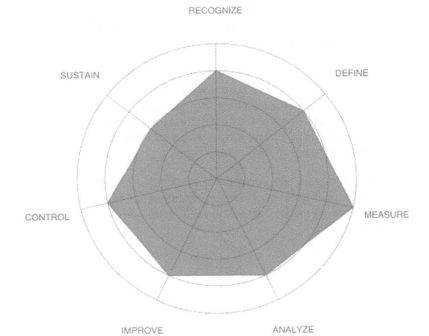

Recruitment Process Outsourcing RPO Scorecard

Your Scores:

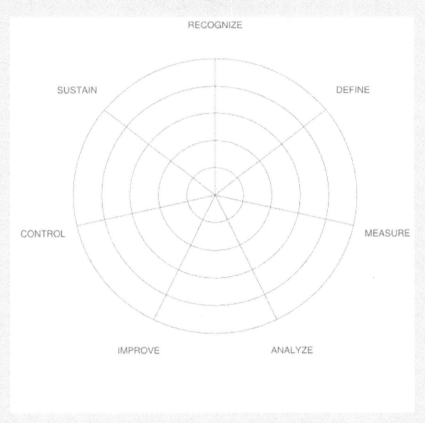

BEGINNING OF THE SELF-ASSESSMENT:

CRITERION #1: RECOGNIZE

INTENT: Be aware of the need for change. Recognize that there is an unfavorable variation, problem or symptom.

In my belief, the answer to this question is clearly defined:

5 Strongly Agree

4 Agree

3 Neutral

2 Disagree

1 Strongly Disagree

1. What are the business objectives to be achieved with Recruitment Process Outsourcing RPO?
<--- Score

2. What prevents me from making the changes I know will make me a more effective Recruitment Process Outsourcing RPO leader?
<--- Score

3. Will a response program recognize when a crisis

occurs and provide some level of response?

<--- Score

4. What do we need to start doing?

<--- Score

5. Who else hopes to benefit from it?

<--- Score

6. How does it fit into our organizational needs and tasks?

<--- Score

7. How do you assess your Recruitment Process Outsourcing RPO workforce capability and capacity needs, including skills, competencies, and staffing levels?

<--- Score

8. Who needs to know about Recruitment Process Outsourcing RPO ?

<--- Score

9. Can Management personnel recognize the monetary benefit of Recruitment Process Outsourcing RPO?

<--- Score

10. What training and capacity building actions are needed to implement proposed reforms?

<--- Score

11. What does Recruitment Process Outsourcing RPO success mean to the stakeholders?

<--- Score

12. Who defines the rules in relation to any given issue?

<--- Score

13. What vendors make products that address the Recruitment Process Outsourcing RPO needs?

<--- Score

14. Think about the people you identified for your Recruitment Process Outsourcing RPO project and the project responsibilities you would assign to them. what kind of training do you think they would need to perform these responsibilities effectively?

<--- Score

15. Does Recruitment Process Outsourcing RPO create potential expectations in other areas that need to be recognized and considered?

<--- Score

16. Cloud management for Recruitment Process Outsourcing RPO do we really need one?

<--- Score

17. What information do users need?

<--- Score

18. Consider your own Recruitment Process Outsourcing RPO project. what types of organizational problems do you think might be causing or affecting your problem, based on the work done so far?

<--- Score

19. Are there any specific expectations or concerns

about the Recruitment Process Outsourcing RPO team, Recruitment Process Outsourcing RPO itself?
<--- Score

20. What problems are you facing and how do you consider Recruitment Process Outsourcing RPO will circumvent those obstacles?
<--- Score

21. What is the smallest subset of the problem we can usefully solve?
<--- Score

22. How are you going to measure success?
<--- Score

23. Do we know what we need to know about this topic?
<--- Score

24. When a Recruitment Process Outsourcing RPO manager recognizes a problem, what options are available?
<--- Score

25. How much are sponsors, customers, partners, stakeholders involved in Recruitment Process Outsourcing RPO? In other words, what are the risks, if Recruitment Process Outsourcing RPO does not deliver successfully?
<--- Score

26. Why do we need to keep records?
<--- Score

27. Will it solve real problems?

<--- Score

28. Will new equipment/products be required to facilitate Recruitment Process Outsourcing RPO delivery for example is new software needed?
<--- Score

29. Does our organization need more Recruitment Process Outsourcing RPO education?
<--- Score

30. What else needs to be measured?
<--- Score

31. How do we Identify specific Recruitment Process Outsourcing RPO investment and emerging trends?
<--- Score

32. How can auditing be a preventative security measure?
<--- Score

33. What situation(s) led to this Recruitment Process Outsourcing RPO Self Assessment?
<--- Score

34. As a sponsor, customer or management, how important is it to meet goals, objectives?
<--- Score

35. What would happen if Recruitment Process Outsourcing RPO weren't done?
<--- Score

36. How are the Recruitment Process Outsourcing RPO's objectives aligned to the organization's overall

business strategy?
<--- Score

37. What should be considered when identifying available resources, constraints, and deadlines?
<--- Score

38. Who had the original idea?
<--- Score

39. Are there Recruitment Process Outsourcing RPO problems defined?
<--- Score

40. For your Recruitment Process Outsourcing RPO project, identify and describe the business environment. is there more than one layer to the business environment?
<--- Score

41. What are the expected benefits of Recruitment Process Outsourcing RPO to the business?
<--- Score

42. Are controls defined to recognize and contain problems?
<--- Score

43. Will Recruitment Process Outsourcing RPO deliverables need to be tested and, if so, by whom?
<--- Score

44. How do you identify the kinds of information that you will need?
<--- Score

45. Is it clear when you think of the day ahead of you what activities and tasks you need to complete?

<--- Score

46. Are there recognized Recruitment Process Outsourcing RPO problems?

<--- Score

47. What tools and technologies are needed for a custom Recruitment Process Outsourcing RPO project?

<--- Score

Add up total points for this section:
_ _ _ _ _ = Total points for this section

Divided by: _ _ _ _ _ _ (number of statements answered) = _ _ _ _ _ _ Average score for this section

Transfer your score to the Recruitment Process Outsourcing RPO Index at the beginning of the Self-Assessment.

CRITERION #2: DEFINE:

INTENT: Formulate the business problem. Define the problem, needs and objectives.

In my belief, the answer to this question is clearly defined:

5 Strongly Agree

4 Agree

3 Neutral

2 Disagree

1 Strongly Disagree

1. Have all of the relationships been defined properly?
<--- Score

2. Is the team adequately staffed with the desired cross-functionality? If not, what additional resources are available to the team?
<--- Score

3. Has the improvement team collected the 'voice of

the customer' (obtained feedback – qualitative and quantitative)?
<--- Score

4. Are approval levels defined for contracts and supplements to contracts?
<--- Score

5. What would be the goal or target for a Recruitment Process Outsourcing RPO's improvement team?
<--- Score

6. Are audit criteria, scope, frequency and methods defined?
<--- Score

7. Has a project plan, Gantt chart, or similar been developed/completed?
<--- Score

8. What are the rough order estimates on cost savings/ opportunities that Recruitment Process Outsourcing RPO brings?
<--- Score

9. Has/have the customer(s) been identified?
<--- Score

10. Will team members regularly document their Recruitment Process Outsourcing RPO work?
<--- Score

11. Is Recruitment Process Outsourcing RPO linked to key business goals and objectives?
<--- Score

12. In what way can we redefine the criteria of choice in our category in our favor, as Method introduced style and design to cleaning and Virgin America returned glamor to flying?
<--- Score

13. How is the team tracking and documenting its work?
<--- Score

14. Are there any constraints known that bear on the ability to perform Recruitment Process Outsourcing RPO work? How is the team addressing them?
<--- Score

15. Will team members perform Recruitment Process Outsourcing RPO work when assigned and in a timely fashion?
<--- Score

16. When is the estimated completion date?
<--- Score

17. In what way can we redefine the criteria of choice clients have in our category in our favor?
<--- Score

18. How and when will the baselines be defined?
<--- Score

19. Who are the Recruitment Process Outsourcing RPO improvement team members, including Management Leads and Coaches?
<--- Score

20. How do you keep key subject matter experts in

the loop?
<--- Score

21. How can the value of Recruitment Process Outsourcing RPO be defined?
<--- Score

22. Is there a completed SIPOC representation, describing the Suppliers, Inputs, Process, Outputs, and Customers?
<--- Score

23. How often are the team meetings?
<--- Score

24. When was the Recruitment Process Outsourcing RPO start date?
<--- Score

25. What are the dynamics of the communication plan?
<--- Score

26. Are task requirements clearly defined?
<--- Score

27. When are meeting minutes sent out? Who is on the distribution list?
<--- Score

28. How did the Recruitment Process Outsourcing RPO manager receive input to the development of a Recruitment Process Outsourcing RPO improvement plan and the estimated completion dates/times of each activity?
<--- Score

29. Is the team equipped with available and reliable resources?
<--- Score

30. How was the 'as is' process map developed, reviewed, verified and validated?
<--- Score

31. Are different versions of process maps needed to account for the different types of inputs?
<--- Score

32. Do we all define Recruitment Process Outsourcing RPO in the same way?
<--- Score

33. What specifically is the problem? Where does it occur? When does it occur? What is its extent?
<--- Score

34. Is it clearly defined in and to your organization what you do?
<--- Score

35. Is data collected and displayed to better understand customer(s) critical needs and requirements.
<--- Score

36. Is there regularly 100% attendance at the team meetings? If not, have appointed substitutes attended to preserve cross-functionality and full representation?
<--- Score

37. How will variation in the actual durations of each activity be dealt with to ensure that the expected Recruitment Process Outsourcing RPO results are met?
<--- Score

38. Is there a critical path to deliver Recruitment Process Outsourcing RPO results?
<--- Score

39. Has everyone on the team, including the team leaders, been properly trained?
<--- Score

40. If substitutes have been appointed, have they been briefed on the Recruitment Process Outsourcing RPO goals and received regular communications as to the progress to date?
<--- Score

41. What defines Best in Class?
<--- Score

42. Has anyone else (internal or external to the organization) attempted to solve this problem or a similar one before? If so, what knowledge can be leveraged from these previous efforts?
<--- Score

43. Are team charters developed?
<--- Score

44. Does the team have regular meetings?
<--- Score

45. What constraints exist that might impact the

team?
<--- Score

46. Is a fully trained team formed, supported, and committed to work on the Recruitment Process Outsourcing RPO improvements?
<--- Score

47. Are improvement team members fully trained on Recruitment Process Outsourcing RPO?
<--- Score

48. What are the compelling business reasons for embarking on Recruitment Process Outsourcing RPO?
<--- Score

49. Have specific policy objectives been defined?
<--- Score

50. What are the Roles and Responsibilities for each team member and its leadership? Where is this documented?
<--- Score

51. How will the Recruitment Process Outsourcing RPO team and the organization measure complete success of Recruitment Process Outsourcing RPO?
<--- Score

52. Is Recruitment Process Outsourcing RPO Required?
<--- Score

53. Have the customer needs been translated into specific, measurable requirements? How?
<--- Score

54. What key business process output measure(s) does Recruitment Process Outsourcing RPO leverage and how?
<--- Score

55. Have all basic functions of Recruitment Process Outsourcing RPO been defined?
<--- Score

56. What baselines are required to be defined and managed?
<--- Score

57. What are the boundaries of the scope? What is in bounds and what is not? What is the start point? What is the stop point?
<--- Score

58. Has a high-level 'as is' process map been completed, verified and validated?
<--- Score

59. Is there a Recruitment Process Outsourcing RPO management charter, including business case, problem and goal statements, scope, milestones, roles and responsibilities, communication plan?
<--- Score

60. Is the current 'as is' process being followed? If not, what are the discrepancies?
<--- Score

61. Is the improvement team aware of the different versions of a process: what they think it is vs. what it actually is vs. what it should be vs. what it could be?
<--- Score

62. Is the team sponsored by a champion or business leader?
<--- Score

63. Are customer(s) identified and segmented according to their different needs and requirements?
<--- Score

64. Do the problem and goal statements meet the SMART criteria (specific, measurable, attainable, relevant, and time-bound)?
<--- Score

65. What critical content must be communicated – who, what, when, where, and how?
<--- Score

66. Is there a completed, verified, and validated high-level 'as is' (not 'should be' or 'could be') business process map?
<--- Score

67. How does the Recruitment Process Outsourcing RPO manager ensure against scope creep?
<--- Score

68. Who defines (or who defined) the rules and roles?
<--- Score

69. Are Required Metrics Defined?
<--- Score

70. Has a team charter been developed and communicated?
<--- Score

71. Are there different segments of customers?
<--- Score

72. How would you define the culture here?
<--- Score

73. Are accountability and ownership for Recruitment Process Outsourcing RPO clearly defined?
<--- Score

74. Are customers identified and high impact areas defined?
<--- Score

75. Are business processes mapped?
<--- Score

76. What customer feedback methods were used to solicit their input?
<--- Score

77. How would one define Recruitment Process Outsourcing RPO leadership?
<--- Score

78. Is full participation by members in regularly held team meetings guaranteed?
<--- Score

79. Has the direction changed at all during the course of Recruitment Process Outsourcing RPO? If so, when did it change and why?
<--- Score

80. Is the scope of Recruitment Process Outsourcing

RPO defined?
<--- Score

81. Is the team formed and are team leaders (Coaches and Management Leads) assigned?
<--- Score

82. What is the minimum educational requirement for potential new hires?
<--- Score

83. Is the Recruitment Process Outsourcing RPO scope manageable?
<--- Score

84. Are roles and responsibilities formally defined?
<--- Score

85. Has the Recruitment Process Outsourcing RPO work been fairly and/or equitably divided and delegated among team members who are qualified and capable to perform the work? Has everyone contributed?
<--- Score

86. Is Recruitment Process Outsourcing RPO currently on schedule according to the plan?
<--- Score

Add up total points for this section:
_ _ _ _ _ = Total points for this section

Divided by: _ _ _ _ _ _ (number of statements answered) = _ _ _ _ _ _
Average score for this section

Transfer your score to the Recruitment
Process Outsourcing RPO Index at the
beginning of the Self-Assessment.

CRITERION #3: MEASURE:

INTENT: Gather the correct data.
Measure the current performance and
evolution of the situation.

In my belief, the answer to this
question is clearly defined:

5 Strongly Agree

4 Agree

3 Neutral

2 Disagree

1 Strongly Disagree

1. What particular quality tools did the team find helpful in establishing measurements?
<--- Score

2. How is progress measured?
<--- Score

3. How will your organization measure success?
<--- Score

4. How will you measure your Recruitment Process Outsourcing RPO effectiveness?
<--- Score

5. Are process variation components displayed/ communicated using suitable charts, graphs, plots?
<--- Score

6. What measurements are possible, practicable and meaningful?
<--- Score

7. Is data collection planned and executed?
<--- Score

8. Is there a Performance Baseline?
<--- Score

9. How do your measurements capture actionable Recruitment Process Outsourcing RPO information for use in exceeding your customers expectations and securing your customers engagement?
<--- Score

10. Are there measurements based on task performance?
<--- Score

11. How is Knowledge Management Measured?
<--- Score

12. When is Knowledge Management Measured?
<--- Score

13. Is performance measured?

<--- Score

14. Are you taking your company in the direction of better and revenue or cheaper and cost?
<--- Score

15. Is key measure data collection planned and executed, process variation displayed and communicated and performance baselined?
<--- Score

16. How can you measure Recruitment Process Outsourcing RPO in a systematic way?
<--- Score

17. Schedule Development, Feasibility Analysis, Recruitment Process Outsourcing RPO Management, Project Closings, Technique: Using the Critical Path Method
<--- Score

18. What are the types and number of measures to use?
<--- Score

19. What are your key Recruitment Process Outsourcing RPO organizational performance measures, including key short and longer-term financial measures?
<--- Score

20. Do we aggressively reward and promote the people who have the biggest impact on creating excellent Recruitment Process Outsourcing RPO services/products?
<--- Score

21. What evidence is there and what is measured?
<--- Score

22. Who should receive measurement reports ?
<--- Score

23. Is data collected on key measures that were identified?
<--- Score

24. How is the value delivered by Recruitment Process Outsourcing RPO being measured?
<--- Score

25. Is a solid data collection plan established that includes measurement systems analysis?
<--- Score

26. What is the total cost related to deploying Recruitment Process Outsourcing RPO, including any consulting or professional services?
<--- Score

27. Are there any easy-to-implement alternatives to Recruitment Process Outsourcing RPO? Sometimes other solutions are available that do not require the cost implications of a full-blown project?
<--- Score

28. Do we effectively measure and reward individual and team performance?
<--- Score

29. How large is the gap between current performance and the customer-specified (goal)

performance?
<--- Score

30. Are the measurements objective?
<--- Score

31. What is measured?
<--- Score

32. Which customers can't participate in our market because they lack skills, wealth, or convenient access to existing solutions?
<--- Score

33. How to measure lifecycle phases?
<--- Score

34. Are high impact defects defined and identified in the business process?
<--- Score

35. Is Process Variation Displayed/Communicated?
<--- Score

36. What measurements are being captured?
<--- Score

37. Why should we expend time and effort to implement measurement?
<--- Score

38. What will be measured?
<--- Score

39. What should be measured?
<--- Score

40. Are the units of measure consistent?
<--- Score

41. The approach of traditional Recruitment Process Outsourcing RPO works for detail complexity but is focused on a systematic approach rather than an understanding of the nature of systems themselves. what approach will permit us to deal with the kind of unpredictable emergent behaviors that dynamic complexity can introduce?
<--- Score

42. Does the practice systematically track and analyze outcomes related for accountability and quality improvement?
<--- Score

43. What is an unallowable cost?
<--- Score

44. Are key measures identified and agreed upon?
<--- Score

45. What about Recruitment Process Outsourcing RPO Analysis of results?
<--- Score

46. How will effects be measured?
<--- Score

47. Are losses documented, analyzed, and remedial processes developed to prevent future losses?
<--- Score

48. What are the agreed upon definitions of the high impact areas, defect(s), unit(s), and opportunities that will figure into the process capability metrics?
<--- Score

49. How are you going to measure success?
<--- Score

50. Does Recruitment Process Outsourcing RPO systematically track and analyze outcomes for accountability and quality improvement?
<--- Score

51. Who participated in the data collection for measurements?
<--- Score

52. What are measures?
<--- Score

53. Can We Measure the Return on Analysis?
<--- Score

54. Do staff have the necessary skills to collect, analyze, and report data?
<--- Score

55. Where is it measured?
<--- Score

56. Which Stakeholder Characteristics Are Analyzed?
<--- Score

57. Does Recruitment Process Outsourcing RPO analysis isolate the fundamental causes of problems?

<--- Score

58. Why Measure?
<--- Score

59. Is this an issue for analysis or intuition?
<--- Score

60. How do we focus on what is right -not who is right?
<--- Score

61. What methods are feasible and acceptable to estimate the impact of reforms?
<--- Score

62. What are our key indicators that you will measure, analyze and track?
<--- Score

63. Is the solution cost-effective?
<--- Score

64. What to measure and why?
<--- Score

65. Will We Aggregate Measures across Priorities?
<--- Score

66. Are we taking our company in the direction of better and revenue or cheaper and cost?
<--- Score

67. How to measure variability?
<--- Score

68. Have the types of risks that may impact Recruitment Process Outsourcing RPO been identified and analyzed?
<--- Score

69. Was a data collection plan established?
<--- Score

70. How Will We Measure Success?
<--- Score

71. What are the key input variables? What are the key process variables? What are the key output variables?
<--- Score

72. What potential environmental factors impact the Recruitment Process Outsourcing RPO effort?
<--- Score

73. Have changes been properly/adequately analyzed for effect?
<--- Score

74. How are measurements made?
<--- Score

75. Among the Recruitment Process Outsourcing RPO product and service cost to be estimated, which is considered hardest to estimate?
<--- Score

76. How do we do risk analysis of rare, cascading, catastrophic events?
<--- Score

77. What are my customers expectations and

measures?
<--- Score

78. Meeting the challenge: are missed Recruitment Process Outsourcing RPO opportunities costing us money?
<--- Score

79. Is it possible to estimate the impact of unanticipated complexity such as wrong or failed assumptions, feedback, etc. on proposed reforms?
<--- Score

80. Have all non-recommended alternatives been analyzed in sufficient detail?
<--- Score

81. Does Recruitment Process Outsourcing RPO analysis show the relationships among important Recruitment Process Outsourcing RPO factors?
<--- Score

82. Have you found any 'ground fruit' or 'low-hanging fruit' for immediate remedies to the gap in performance?
<--- Score

83. How frequently do you track Recruitment Process Outsourcing RPO measures?
<--- Score

84. Which customers cant participate in our Recruitment Process Outsourcing RPO domain because they lack skills, wealth, or convenient access to existing solutions?
<--- Score

85. Does the Recruitment Process Outsourcing RPO task fit the client's priorities?
<--- Score

86. How frequently do we track measures?
<--- Score

87. What are the costs of reform?
<--- Score

88. What charts has the team used to display the components of variation in the process?
<--- Score

89. How do you measure success?
<--- Score

90. Can we do Recruitment Process Outsourcing RPO without complex (expensive) analysis?
<--- Score

91. What data was collected (past, present, future/ ongoing)?
<--- Score

92. What Relevant Entities could be measured?
<--- Score

93. What key measures identified indicate the performance of the business process?
<--- Score

94. Why identify and analyze stakeholders and their interests?
<--- Score

95. Customer Measures: How Do Customers See Us?
<--- Score

96. What is the right balance of time and resources between investigation, analysis, and discussion and dissemination?
<--- Score

97. Why do measure/indicators matter?
<--- Score

98. Why do the measurements/indicators matter?
<--- Score

99. How can we measure the performance?
<--- Score

100. Is long term and short term variability accounted for?
<--- Score

101. Have the concerns of stakeholders to help identify and define potential barriers been obtained and analyzed?
<--- Score

102. How will success or failure be measured?
<--- Score

103. Will Recruitment Process Outsourcing RPO have an impact on current business continuity, disaster recovery processes and/or infrastructure?
<--- Score

104. What has the team done to assure the stability

and accuracy of the measurement process?
<--- Score

105. How will measures be used to manage and adapt?
<--- Score

106. What are the uncertainties surrounding estimates of impact?
<--- Score

107. How do you identify and analyze stakeholders and their interests?
<--- Score

Add up total points for this section:
_ _ _ _ _ = Total points for this section

Divided by: _ _ _ _ _ _ (number of statements answered) = _ _ _ _ _ _
Average score for this section

Transfer your score to the Recruitment Process Outsourcing RPO Index at the beginning of the Self-Assessment.

CRITERION #4: ANALYZE:

INTENT: Analyze causes, assumptions
and hypotheses.

In my belief, the answer to this
question is clearly defined:

5 Strongly Agree

4 Agree

3 Neutral

2 Disagree

1 Strongly Disagree

1. A compounding model resolution with available relevant data can often provide insight towards a solution methodology; which Recruitment Process Outsourcing RPO models, tools and techniques are necessary?
<--- Score

2. How do we promote understanding that opportunity for improvement is not criticism of the status quo, or the people who created the

status quo?
<--- Score

3. What were the financial benefits resulting from any 'ground fruit or low-hanging fruit' (quick fixes)?
<--- Score

4. Was a detailed process map created to amplify critical steps of the 'as is' business process?
<--- Score

5. Record-keeping requirements flow from the records needed as inputs, outputs, controls and for transformation of a Recruitment Process Outsourcing RPO process. ask yourself: are the records needed as inputs to the Recruitment Process Outsourcing RPO process available?
<--- Score

6. Were Pareto charts (or similar) used to portray the 'heavy hitters' (or key sources of variation)?
<--- Score

7. What successful thing are we doing today that may be blinding us to new growth opportunities?
<--- Score

8. How often will data be collected for measures?
<--- Score

9. Is Data and process analysis, root cause analysis and quantifying the gap/opportunity in place?
<--- Score

10. What are your current levels and trends in key Recruitment Process Outsourcing RPO measures

or indicators of product and process performance that are important to and directly serve your customers?

<--- Score

11. Is the suppliers process defined and controlled?

<--- Score

12. Have any additional benefits been identified that will result from closing all or most of the gaps?

<--- Score

13. How do you use Recruitment Process Outsourcing RPO data and information to support organizational decision making and innovation?

<--- Score

14. Have the problem and goal statements been updated to reflect the additional knowledge gained from the analyze phase?

<--- Score

15. What are the best opportunities for value improvement?

<--- Score

16. Were any designed experiments used to generate additional insight into the data analysis?

<--- Score

17. Do you, as a leader, bounce back quickly from setbacks?

<--- Score

18. Do your employees have the opportunity to do

what they do best everyday?
<--- Score

19. What does the data say about the performance of the business process?
<--- Score

20. What were the crucial 'moments of truth' on the process map?
<--- Score

21. What other jobs or tasks affect the performance of the steps in the Recruitment Process Outsourcing RPO process?
<--- Score

22. Where is the data coming from to measure compliance?
<--- Score

23. What controls do we have in place to protect data?
<--- Score

24. What tools were used to generate the list of possible causes?
<--- Score

25. What quality tools were used to get through the analyze phase?
<--- Score

26. What is the cost of poor quality as supported by the team's analysis?
<--- Score

27. What other organizational variables, such as

reward systems or communication systems, affect the performance of this Recruitment Process Outsourcing RPO process?

<--- Score

28. What are the revised rough estimates of the financial savings/opportunity for Recruitment Process Outsourcing RPO improvements?

<--- Score

29. What conclusions were drawn from the team's data collection and analysis? How did the team reach these conclusions?

<--- Score

30. How do you measure the Operational performance of your key work systems and processes, including productivity, cycle time, and other appropriate measures of process effectiveness, efficiency, and innovation?

<--- Score

31. Think about the functions involved in your Recruitment Process Outsourcing RPO project. what processes flow from these functions?

<--- Score

32. Is the performance gap determined?

<--- Score

33. Was a cause-and-effect diagram used to explore the different types of causes (or sources of variation)?

<--- Score

34. Identify an operational issue in your organization. for example, could a particular task

be done more quickly or more efficiently?
<--- Score

35. Did any value-added analysis or 'lean thinking' take place to identify some of the gaps shown on the 'as is' process map?
<--- Score

36. What process should we select for improvement?
<--- Score

37. How is the way you as the leader think and process information affecting your organizational culture?
<--- Score

38. What are your current levels and trends in key measures or indicators of Recruitment Process Outsourcing RPO product and process performance that are important to and directly serve your customers? how do these results compare with the performance of your competitors and other organizations with similar offerings?
<--- Score

39. What are the disruptive Recruitment Process Outsourcing RPO technologies that enable our organization to radically change our business processes?
<--- Score

40. When conducting a business process reengineering study, what should we look for when trying to identify business processes to change?
<--- Score

41. Think about some of the processes you undertake within your organization. which do you own?
<--- Score

42. How do mission and objectives affect the Recruitment Process Outsourcing RPO processes of our organization?
<--- Score

43. Did any additional data need to be collected?
<--- Score

44. Is the gap/opportunity displayed and communicated in financial terms?
<--- Score

45. Are gaps between current performance and the goal performance identified?
<--- Score

46. Teaches and consults on quality process improvement, project management, and accelerated Recruitment Process Outsourcing RPO techniques
<--- Score

47. What did the team gain from developing a sub-process map?
<--- Score

48. Do our leaders quickly bounce back from setbacks?
<--- Score

49. What tools were used to narrow the list of possible

causes?
<--- Score

50. Were there any improvement opportunities identified from the process analysis?
<--- Score

51. Is the Recruitment Process Outsourcing RPO process severely broken such that a re-design is necessary?
<--- Score

52. What are our Recruitment Process Outsourcing RPO Processes?
<--- Score

53. How does the organization define, manage, and improve its Recruitment Process Outsourcing RPO processes?
<--- Score

54. Can we add value to the current Recruitment Process Outsourcing RPO decision-making process (largely qualitative) by incorporating uncertainty modeling (more quantitative)?
<--- Score

55. An organizationally feasible system request is one that considers the mission, goals and objectives of the organization. key questions are: is the solution request practical and will it solve a problem or take advantage of an opportunity to achieve company goals?
<--- Score

56. How was the detailed process map generated,

verified, and validated?
<--- Score

Add up total points for this section:
_____ = Total points for this section

Divided by: _____ (number of
statements answered) = _____
Average score for this section

Transfer your score to the Recruitment
Process Outsourcing RPO Index at the
beginning of the Self-Assessment.

CRITERION #5: IMPROVE:

INTENT: Develop a practical solution.
Innovate, establish and test the
solution and to measure the results.

In my belief, the answer to this
question is clearly defined:

5 Strongly Agree

4 Agree

3 Neutral

2 Disagree

1 Strongly Disagree

1. Are there any constraints (technical, political,
cultural, or otherwise) that would inhibit certain
solutions?
<--- Score

2. What is the team's contingency plan for potential
problems occurring in implementation?
<--- Score

3. Who will be using the results of the measurement activities?
<--- Score

4. Can the solution be designed and implemented within an acceptable time period?
<--- Score

5. Are possible solutions generated and tested?
<--- Score

6. What is Recruitment Process Outsourcing RPO's impact on utilizing the best solution(s)?
<--- Score

7. How will you know when its improved?
<--- Score

8. Is pilot data collected and analyzed?
<--- Score

9. What needs improvement?
<--- Score

10. How do you improve your likelihood of success ?
<--- Score

11. What does the 'should be' process map/design look like?
<--- Score

12. What error proofing will be done to address some of the discrepancies observed in the 'as is' process?
<--- Score

13. What is the implementation plan?

<--- Score

14. Who controls the risk?
<--- Score

15. How can we improve performance?
<--- Score

16. Who will be responsible for making the decisions
to include or exclude requested changes once
Recruitment Process Outsourcing RPO is underway?
<--- Score

**17. How do you manage and improve your
Recruitment Process Outsourcing RPO work
systems to deliver customer value and achieve
organizational success and sustainability?**
<--- Score

18. Does the goal represent a desired result that can
be measured?
<--- Score

19. Are we Assessing Recruitment Process
Outsourcing RPO and Risk?
<--- Score

**20. At what point will vulnerability assessments be
performed once Recruitment Process Outsourcing
RPO is put into production (e.g., ongoing Risk
Management after implementation)?**
<--- Score

21. How do we measure risk?
<--- Score

22. Are the best solutions selected?
<--- Score

23. How will the organization know that the solution worked?
<--- Score

24. Are new and improved process ('should be') maps developed?
<--- Score

25. How will you measure the results?
<--- Score

26. What improvements have been achieved?
<--- Score

27. Is there a small-scale pilot for proposed improvement(s)? What conclusions were drawn from the outcomes of a pilot?
<--- Score

28. What do we want to improve?
<--- Score

29. Describe the design of the pilot and what tests were conducted, if any?
<--- Score

30. Was a pilot designed for the proposed solution(s)?
<--- Score

31. How do we measure improved Recruitment Process Outsourcing RPO service perception, and satisfaction?
<--- Score

32. Is Supporting Recruitment Process Outsourcing RPO documentation required?

<--- Score

33. Risk factors: what are the characteristics of Recruitment Process Outsourcing RPO that make it risky?

<--- Score

34. How important is the completion of a recognized college or graduate-level degree program in the hiring decision?

<--- Score

35. What is the magnitude of the improvements?

<--- Score

36. How do we keep improving Recruitment Process Outsourcing RPO?

<--- Score

37. For decision problems, how do you develop a decision statement?

<--- Score

38. How will you know that you have improved?

<--- Score

39. What to do with the results or outcomes of measurements?

<--- Score

40. What is the risk?

<--- Score

41. What were the underlying assumptions on the cost-benefit analysis?
<--- Score

42. Explorations of the frontiers of Recruitment Process Outsourcing RPO will help you build influence, improve Recruitment Process Outsourcing RPO, optimize decision making, and sustain change
<--- Score

43. Is there a high likelihood that any recommendations will achieve their intended results?
<--- Score

44. Is a solution implementation plan established, including schedule/work breakdown structure, resources, risk management plan, cost/budget, and control plan?
<--- Score

45. How to Improve?
<--- Score

46. How can we improve Recruitment Process Outsourcing RPO?
<--- Score

47. How do the Recruitment Process Outsourcing RPO results compare with the performance of your competitors and other organizations with similar offerings?
<--- Score

48. Do we combine technical expertise with business knowledge and Recruitment Process Outsourcing

RPO Key topics include lifecycles, development approaches, requirements and how to make a business case?

<--- Score

49. What tools were most useful during the improve phase?

<--- Score

50. What should a proof of concept or pilot accomplish?

<--- Score

51. How does the solution remove the key sources of issues discovered in the analyze phase?

<--- Score

52. How Do We Link Measurement and Risk?

<--- Score

53. Is the solution technically practical?

<--- Score

54. If you could go back in time five years, what decision would you make differently? What is your best guess as to what decision you're making today you might regret five years from now?

<--- Score

55. How will the team or the process owner(s) monitor the implementation plan to see that it is working as intended?

<--- Score

56. How did the team generate the list of possible solutions?

<--- Score

57. What actually has to improve and by how much?
<--- Score

58. Is the optimal solution selected based on testing and analysis?
<--- Score

59. Is the measure understandable to a variety of people?
<--- Score

60. For estimation problems, how do you develop an estimation statement?
<--- Score

61. How do we go about Comparing Recruitment Process Outsourcing RPO approaches/solutions?
<--- Score

62. What tools were used to evaluate the potential solutions?
<--- Score

63. How do we improve productivity?
<--- Score

64. How does the team improve its work?
<--- Score

65. Why improve in the first place?
<--- Score

66. How do we decide how much to remunerate an

employee?
<--- Score

67. How do you measure progress and evaluate training effectiveness?
<--- Score

68. How significant is the improvement in the eyes of the end user?
<--- Score

69. What tools were used to tap into the creativity and encourage 'outside the box' thinking?
<--- Score

70. What communications are necessary to support the implementation of the solution?
<--- Score

71. Is there a cost/benefit analysis of optimal solution(s)?
<--- Score

72. Risk events: what are the things that could go wrong?
<--- Score

73. What is the Recruitment Process Outsourcing RPO sustainability risk?
<--- Score

74. What are the implications of this decision 10 minutes, 10 months, and 10 years from now?
<--- Score

75. In the past few months, what is the smallest

change we have made that has had the biggest positive result? What was it about that small change that produced the large return?
<--- Score

76. What lessons, if any, from a pilot were incorporated into the design of the full-scale solution?
<--- Score

77. What attendant changes will need to be made to ensure that the solution is successful?
<--- Score

78. Were any criteria developed to assist the team in testing and evaluating potential solutions?
<--- Score

79. How will we know that a change is improvement?
<--- Score

80. What tools do you use once you have decided on a Recruitment Process Outsourcing RPO strategy and more importantly how do you choose?
<--- Score

81. Who controls key decisions that will be made?
<--- Score

82. What went well, what should change, what can improve?
<--- Score

83. What can we do to improve?
<--- Score

84. What resources are required for the improvement effort?
<--- Score

85. Do we cover the five essential competencies- Communication, Collaboration,Innovation, Adaptability, and Leadership that improve an organization's ability to leverage the new Recruitment Process Outsourcing RPO in a volatile global economy?
<--- Score

86. Who are the people involved in developing and implementing Recruitment Process Outsourcing RPO?
<--- Score

87. Are we using Recruitment Process Outsourcing RPO to communicate information about our Cybersecurity Risk Management programs including the effectiveness of those programs to stakeholders, including boards, investors, auditors, and insurers?
<--- Score

88. How do we Improve Recruitment Process Outsourcing RPO service perception, and satisfaction?
<--- Score

89. What evaluation strategy is needed and what needs to be done to assure its implementation and use?
<--- Score

90. How can skill-level changes improve Recruitment Process Outsourcing RPO?

<--- Score

91. To what extent does management recognize Recruitment Process Outsourcing RPO as a tool to increase the results?
<--- Score

92. Who will be responsible for documenting the Recruitment Process Outsourcing RPO requirements in detail?
<--- Score

93. Is the implementation plan designed?
<--- Score

94. Are improved process ('should be') maps modified based on pilot data and analysis?
<--- Score

95. Is a contingency plan established?
<--- Score

Add up total points for this section:
_____ = Total points for this section

Divided by: _____ (number of statements answered) = _____
Average score for this section

Transfer your score to the Recruitment Process Outsourcing RPO Index at the beginning of the Self-Assessment.

CRITERION #6: CONTROL:

INTENT: Implement the practical solution. Maintain the performance and correct possible complications.

In my belief, the answer to this question is clearly defined:

5 Strongly Agree

4 Agree

3 Neutral

2 Disagree

1 Strongly Disagree

1. How will input, process, and output variables be checked to detect for sub-optimal conditions?
<--- Score

2. Against what alternative is success being measured?
<--- Score

3. Is there a recommended audit plan for routine

surveillance inspections of Recruitment Process Outsourcing RPO's gains?
<--- Score

4. What other areas of the organization might benefit from the Recruitment Process Outsourcing RPO team's improvements, knowledge, and learning?
<--- Score

5. Will any special training be provided for results interpretation?
<--- Score

6. Strategic planning -Recruitment Process Outsourcing RPO relations
<--- Score

7. Whats the best design framework for Recruitment Process Outsourcing RPO organization now that, in a post industrial-age if the top-down, command and control model is no longer relevant?
<--- Score

8. Can Recruitment Process Outsourcing RPO be learned?
<--- Score

9. How will the process owner verify improvement in present and future sigma levels, process capabilities?
<--- Score

10. How likely is the current Recruitment Process Outsourcing RPO plan to come in on schedule or on budget?
<--- Score

11. Does the Recruitment Process Outsourcing RPO performance meet the customer's requirements?
<--- Score

12. What are the known security controls?
<--- Score

13. Is new knowledge gained imbedded in the response plan?
<--- Score

14. What do we stand for--and what are we against?
<--- Score

15. Is there a documented and implemented monitoring plan?
<--- Score

16. Does a troubleshooting guide exist or is it needed?
<--- Score

17. What are the key elements of your Recruitment Process Outsourcing RPO performance improvement system, including your evaluation, organizational learning, and innovation processes?
<--- Score

18. Who controls critical resources?
<--- Score

19. In the case of a Recruitment Process Outsourcing RPO project, the criteria for the audit derive from implementation objectives.

an audit of a Recruitment Process Outsourcing RPO project involves assessing whether the recommendations outlined for implementation have been met. Can we track that any Recruitment Process Outsourcing RPO project is implemented as planned, and is it working?
<--- Score

20. Do you monitor the effectiveness of your Recruitment Process Outsourcing RPO activities?
<--- Score

21. Are documented procedures clear and easy to follow for the operators?
<--- Score

22. What is your theory of human motivation, and how does your compensation plan fit with that view?
<--- Score

23. Are pertinent alerts monitored, analyzed and distributed to appropriate personnel?
<--- Score

24. What is the control/monitoring plan?
<--- Score

25. Who will be in control?
<--- Score

26. Measure, Monitor and Predict Recruitment Process Outsourcing RPO Activities to Optimize Operations and Profitably, and Enhance Outcomes
<--- Score

27. What are we attempting to measure/monitor?

<--- Score

28. What are your results for key measures or indicators of the accomplishment of your Recruitment Process Outsourcing RPO strategy and action plans, including building and strengthening core competencies?
<--- Score

29. Where do ideas that reach policy makers and planners as proposals for Recruitment Process Outsourcing RPO strengthening and reform actually originate?
<--- Score

30. What is the recommended frequency of auditing?
<--- Score

31. Are suggested corrective/restorative actions indicated on the response plan for known causes to problems that might surface?
<--- Score

32. Implementation Planning- is a pilot needed to test the changes before a full roll out occurs?
<--- Score

33. What quality tools were useful in the control phase?
<--- Score

34. What key inputs and outputs are being measured on an ongoing basis?
<--- Score

35. Is a response plan in place for when the input,

process, or output measures indicate an 'out-of-control' condition?
<--- Score

36. Why is change control necessary?
<--- Score

37. What can you control?
<--- Score

38. Does Recruitment Process Outsourcing RPO appropriately measure and monitor risk?
<--- Score

39. Is there a standardized process?
<--- Score

40. Are there documented procedures?
<--- Score

41. What are the critical parameters to watch?
<--- Score

42. How can we best use all of our knowledge repositories to enhance learning and sharing?
<--- Score

43. Is there a Recruitment Process Outsourcing RPO Communication plan covering who needs to get what information when?
<--- Score

44. Have new or revised work instructions resulted?
<--- Score

45. Are operating procedures consistent?

<--- Score

46. What is our theory of human motivation, and how does our compensation plan fit with that view?
<--- Score

47. Who is the Recruitment Process Outsourcing RPO process owner?
<--- Score

48. How will the day-to-day responsibilities for monitoring and continual improvement be transferred from the improvement team to the process owner?
<--- Score

49. Are controls in place and consistently applied?
<--- Score

50. How might the organization capture best practices and lessons learned so as to leverage improvements across the business?
<--- Score

51. How do you select, collect, align, and integrate Recruitment Process Outsourcing RPO data and information for tracking daily operations and overall organizational performance, including progress relative to strategic objectives and action plans?
<--- Score

52. Is reporting being used or needed?
<--- Score

53. Does job training on the documented procedures need to be part of the process team's education and training?
<--- Score

54. What should the next improvement project be that is related to Recruitment Process Outsourcing RPO?
<--- Score

55. How will the process owner and team be able to hold the gains?
<--- Score

56. Are new process steps, standards, and documentation ingrained into normal operations?
<--- Score

57. What should we measure to verify effectiveness gains?
<--- Score

58. Does the response plan contain a definite closed loop continual improvement scheme (e.g., plan-do-check-act)?
<--- Score

59. What should we measure to verify efficiency gains?
<--- Score

60. Were the planned controls in place?
<--- Score

61. Is there a transfer of ownership and knowledge to process owner and process team tasked with the

responsibilities.
<--- Score

62. How will report readings be checked to effectively monitor performance?
<--- Score

63. How do controls support value?
<--- Score

64. Is knowledge gained on process shared and institutionalized?
<--- Score

65. Were the planned controls working?
<--- Score

66. How will new or emerging customer needs/ requirements be checked/communicated to orient the process toward meeting the new specifications and continually reducing variation?
<--- Score

67. How do our controls stack up?
<--- Score

68. Is there documentation that will support the successful operation of the improvement?
<--- Score

69. Who has control over resources?
<--- Score

70. Has the improved process and its steps been standardized?
<--- Score

71. Do the decisions we make today help people and the planet tomorrow?
<--- Score

72. What other systems, operations, processes, and infrastructures (hiring practices, staffing, training, incentives/rewards, metrics/dashboards/scorecards, etc.) need updates, additions, changes, or deletions in order to facilitate knowledge transfer and improvements?
<--- Score

73. Is a response plan established and deployed?
<--- Score

74. Recruitment Process Outsourcing RPO in management -Strategic planning
<--- Score

75. Do we monitor the Recruitment Process Outsourcing RPO decisions made and fine tune them as they evolve?
<--- Score

76. Will existing staff require re-training, for example, to learn new business processes?
<--- Score

77. How do you encourage people to take control and responsibility?
<--- Score

78. Is there a control plan in place for sustaining improvements (short and long-term)?
<--- Score

79. Do the Recruitment Process Outsourcing RPO decisions we make today help people and the planet tomorrow?

<--- Score

Add up total points for this section:

_ _ _ _ _ = Total points for this section

Divided by: _ _ _ _ _ _ (number of statements answered) = _ _ _ _ _ _
Average score for this section

Transfer your score to the Recruitment Process Outsourcing RPO Index at the beginning of the Self-Assessment.

CRITERION #7: SUSTAIN:

INTENT: Retain the benefits.

In my belief, the answer to this question is clearly defined:

5 Strongly Agree

4 Agree

3 Neutral

2 Disagree

1 Strongly Disagree

1. How do we foster the skills, knowledge, talents, attributes, and characteristics we want to have?
<--- Score

2. Are we making progress? and are we making progress as Recruitment Process Outsourcing RPO leaders?
<--- Score

3. If we got kicked out and the board brought in a new CEO, what would he do?
<--- Score

4. What are the challenges?
<--- Score

5. Is it economical; do we have the time and money?
<--- Score

6. Who is On the Team?
<--- Score

7. Operational - will it work?
<--- Score

8. What are we challenging, in the sense that Mac challenged the PC or Dove tackled the Beauty Myth?
<--- Score

9. Which criteria are used to determine which projects are going to be pursued or discarded?
<--- Score

10. Why are Recruitment Process Outsourcing RPO skills important?
<--- Score

11. What is an unauthorized commitment?
<--- Score

12. Is there any reason to believe the opposite of my current belief?
<--- Score

13. How to deal with Recruitment Process Outsourcing RPO Changes?
<--- Score

14. Will there be any necessary staff changes (redundancies or new hires)?
<--- Score

15. Is there any existing Recruitment Process Outsourcing RPO governance structure?
<--- Score

16. How can you negotiate Recruitment Process Outsourcing RPO successfully with a stubborn boss, an irate client, or a deceitful coworker?
<--- Score

17. What is Tricky About This?
<--- Score

18. Which Recruitment Process Outsourcing RPO goals are the most important?
<--- Score

19. What are the long-term Recruitment Process Outsourcing RPO goals?
<--- Score

20. Did my employees make progress today?
<--- Score

21. Think of your Recruitment Process Outsourcing RPO project. what are the main functions?
<--- Score

22. What are strategies for increasing support and reducing opposition?
<--- Score

23. How do we manage Recruitment Process Outsourcing RPO Knowledge Management (KM)?
<--- Score

24. Are we relevant? Will we be relevant five years from now? Ten?
<--- Score

25. What is our competitive advantage?
<--- Score

26. How are we doing compared to our industry?
<--- Score

27. What counts that we are not counting?
<--- Score

28. If you had to rebuild your organization without any traditional competitive advantages (i.e., no killer a technology, promising research, innovative product/service delivery model, etc.), how would your people have to approach their work and collaborate together in order to create the necessary conditions for success?
<--- Score

29. What management system can we use to leverage the Recruitment Process Outsourcing RPO experience, ideas, and concerns of the people closest to the work to be done?
<--- Score

30. Who do we want our customers to become?
<--- Score

31. What business benefits will Recruitment Process

Outsourcing RPO goals deliver if achieved?
<--- Score

32. Who will manage the integration of tools?
<--- Score

33. When information truly is ubiquitous, when reach and connectivity are completely global, when computing resources are infinite, and when a whole new set of impossibilities are not only possible, but happening, what will that do to our business?
<--- Score

34. Is Recruitment Process Outsourcing RPO dependent on the successful delivery of a current project?
<--- Score

35. Design Thinking: Integrating Innovation, Recruitment Process Outsourcing RPO Experience, and Brand Value
<--- Score

36. How do we accomplish our long range Recruitment Process Outsourcing RPO goals?
<--- Score

37. What are the business goals Recruitment Process Outsourcing RPO is aiming to achieve?
<--- Score

38. Who else should we help?
<--- Score

39. Do I know what I'm doing? And who do I call if I don't?

<--- Score

40. Do we have the right capabilities and capacities?
<--- Score

41. What stupid rule would we most like to kill?
<--- Score

42. What is our formula for success in Recruitment Process Outsourcing RPO ?
<--- Score

43. Where is our petri dish?
<--- Score

44. Which functions and people interact with the supplier and or customer?
<--- Score

45. Would you rather sell to knowledgeable and informed customers or to uninformed customers?
<--- Score

46. Design Thinking: Integrating Innovation, Recruitment Process Outsourcing RPO, and Brand Value
<--- Score

47. What will drive Recruitment Process Outsourcing RPO change?
<--- Score

48. In retrospect, of the projects that we pulled the plug on, what percent do we wish had been allowed to keep going, and what percent do we wish had

ended earlier?

<--- Score

49. Is our strategy driving our strategy? Or is the way in which we allocate resources driving our strategy?

<--- Score

50. What are internal and external Recruitment Process Outsourcing RPO relations?

<--- Score

51. If there were zero limitations, what would we do differently?

<--- Score

52. Do we underestimate the customer's journey?

<--- Score

53. What are the critical success factors?

<--- Score

54. Can we maintain our growth without detracting from the factors that have contributed to our success?

<--- Score

55. Who will use it?

<--- Score

56. Do we have the right people on the bus?

<--- Score

57. How to Secure Recruitment Process Outsourcing RPO?

<--- Score

58. How will you know that the Recruitment Process Outsourcing RPO project has been successful?

<--- Score

59. Is there a limit on the number of users in Recruitment Process Outsourcing RPO ?

<--- Score

60. What is our Recruitment Process Outsourcing RPO Strategy?

<--- Score

61. Who will be responsible for deciding whether Recruitment Process Outsourcing RPO goes ahead or not after the initial investigations?

<--- Score

62. If we weren't already in this business, would we enter it today? And if not, what are we going to do about it?

<--- Score

63. How much does Recruitment Process Outsourcing RPO help?

<--- Score

64. What sources do you use to gather information for a Recruitment Process Outsourcing RPO study?

<--- Score

65. Ask yourself: how would we do this work if we only had one staff member to do it?

<--- Score

66. If our customer were my grandmother, would I tell

her to buy what we're selling?
<--- Score

67. Are there any disadvantages to implementing Recruitment Process Outsourcing RPO? There might be some that are less obvious?
<--- Score

68. Schedule -can it be done in the given time?
<--- Score

69. What happens if you do not have enough funding?
<--- Score

70. How will we know if we have been successful?
<--- Score

71. What would have to be true for the option on the table to be the best possible choice?
<--- Score

72. What are the Essentials of Internal Recruitment Process Outsourcing RPO Management?
<--- Score

73. How would our PR, marketing, and social media change if we did not use outside agencies?
<--- Score

74. What is the craziest thing we can do?
<--- Score

75. How do we make it meaningful in connecting Recruitment Process Outsourcing RPO with what users do day-to-day?

<--- Score

76. What are the top 3 things at the forefront of our Recruitment Process Outsourcing RPO agendas for the next 3 years?

<--- Score

77. How is business? Why?

<--- Score

78. Why don't our customers like us?

<--- Score

79. What are the usability implications of Recruitment Process Outsourcing RPO actions?

<--- Score

80. What are your most important goals for the strategic Recruitment Process Outsourcing RPO objectives?

<--- Score

81. Do you have any supplemental information to add to this checklist?

<--- Score

82. Do we say no to customers for no reason?

<--- Score

83. What information is critical to our organization that our executives are ignoring?

<--- Score

84. Are assumptions made in Recruitment Process Outsourcing RPO stated explicitly?

<--- Score

85. Is the Recruitment Process Outsourcing RPO organization completing tasks effectively and efficiently?
<--- Score

86. How can we become the company that would put us out of business?
<--- Score

87. Will it be accepted by users?
<--- Score

88. How does Recruitment Process Outsourcing RPO integrate with other business initiatives?
<--- Score

89. What is it like to work for me?
<--- Score

90. How do we engage the workforce, in addition to satisfying them?
<--- Score

91. What will be the consequences to the stakeholder (financial, reputation etc) if Recruitment Process Outsourcing RPO does not go ahead or fails to deliver the objectives?
<--- Score

92. What current systems have to be understood and/or changed?
<--- Score

93. How can we become more high-tech but still be high touch?

<--- Score

94. What is our question?
<--- Score

95. What was the last experiment we ran?
<--- Score

96. We picked a method, now what?
<--- Score

97. You may have created your customer policies at a time when you lacked resources, technology wasn't up-to-snuff, or low service levels were the industry norm. Have those circumstances changed?
<--- Score

98. Are we / should we be Revolutionary or evolutionary?
<--- Score

99. Who Uses What?
<--- Score

100. Who is the main stakeholder, with ultimate responsibility for driving Recruitment Process Outsourcing RPO forward?
<--- Score

101. Are the criteria for selecting recommendations stated?
<--- Score

102. What is the overall business strategy?
<--- Score

103. What are specific Recruitment Process Outsourcing RPO Rules to follow?
<--- Score

104. What threat is Recruitment Process Outsourcing RPO addressing?
<--- Score

105. Why should people listen to you?
<--- Score

106. How will we insure seamless interoperability of Recruitment Process Outsourcing RPO moving forward?
<--- Score

107. Who are four people whose careers I've enhanced?
<--- Score

108. Political -is anyone trying to undermine this project?
<--- Score

109. How can we incorporate support to ensure safe and effective use of Recruitment Process Outsourcing RPO into the services that we provide?
<--- Score

110. Who will provide the final approval of Recruitment Process Outsourcing RPO deliverables?
<--- Score

111. How do you determine the key elements

that affect Recruitment Process Outsourcing RPO workforce satisfaction? how are these elements determined for different workforce groups and segments?
<--- Score

112. Are there Recruitment Process Outsourcing RPO Models?
<--- Score

113. Is maximizing Recruitment Process Outsourcing RPO protection the same as minimizing Recruitment Process Outsourcing RPO loss?
<--- Score

114. What are the success criteria that will indicate that Recruitment Process Outsourcing RPO objectives have been met and the benefits delivered?
<--- Score

115. Am I failing differently each time?
<--- Score

116. What are the Key enablers to make this Recruitment Process Outsourcing RPO move?
<--- Score

117. How do we Lead with Recruitment Process Outsourcing RPO in Mind?
<--- Score

118. Who sets the Recruitment Process Outsourcing RPO standards?
<--- Score

119. What should we stop doing?

<--- Score

120. Is the impact that Recruitment Process Outsourcing RPO has shown?

<--- Score

121. In what ways are Recruitment Process Outsourcing RPO vendors and us interacting to ensure safe and effective use?

<--- Score

122. Have new benefits been realized?

<--- Score

123. What are the gaps in my knowledge and experience?

<--- Score

124. What is something you believe that nearly no one agrees with you on?

<--- Score

125. What trouble can we get into?

<--- Score

126. Think about the kind of project structure that would be appropriate for your Recruitment Process Outsourcing RPO project. should it be formal and complex, or can it be less formal and relatively simple?

<--- Score

127. What does your signature ensure?

<--- Score

128. If our company went out of business tomorrow, would anyone who doesn't get a paycheck here care?
<--- Score

129. Who do we think the world wants us to be?
<--- Score

130. Do we have enough freaky customers in our portfolio pushing us to the limit day in and day out?
<--- Score

131. Who have we, as a company, historically been when we've been at our best?
<--- Score

132. What is the mission of the organization?
<--- Score

133. How long will it take to change?
<--- Score

134. In the past year, what have you done (or could you have done) to increase the accurate perception of this company/brand as ethical and honest?
<--- Score

135. Do you have a vision statement?
<--- Score

136. Why is it important to have senior management support for a Recruitment Process Outsourcing RPO project?
<--- Score

137. Among our stronger employees, how many see themselves at the company in three years? How

many would leave for a 10 percent raise from another company?

<--- Score

138. Do we think we know, or do we know we know ?

<--- Score

139. What am I trying to prove to myself, and how might it be hijacking my life and business success?

<--- Score

140. Has implementation been effective in reaching specified objectives?

<--- Score

141. What is the purpose of Recruitment Process Outsourcing RPO in relation to the mission?

<--- Score

142. Whom among your colleagues do you trust, and for what?

<--- Score

143. Who will determine interim and final deadlines?

<--- Score

144. What is the range of capabilities?

<--- Score

145. What happens at this company when people fail?

<--- Score

146. Are we changing as fast as the world around us?

<--- Score

147. Is a Recruitment Process Outsourcing RPO Team Work effort in place?
<--- Score

148. Who is responsible for ensuring appropriate resources (time, people and money) are allocated to Recruitment Process Outsourcing RPO?
<--- Score

149. What may be the consequences for the performance of an organization if all stakeholders are not consulted regarding Recruitment Process Outsourcing RPO?
<--- Score

150. How will we ensure we get what we expected?
<--- Score

151. Who is responsible for errors?
<--- Score

152. What new services of functionality will be implemented next with Recruitment Process Outsourcing RPO ?
<--- Score

153. Are you satisfied with your current role? If not, what is missing from it?
<--- Score

154. How do we go about Securing Recruitment Process Outsourcing RPO?
<--- Score

155. What are the short and long-term

Recruitment Process Outsourcing RPO goals?
<--- Score

156. Were lessons learned captured and communicated?
<--- Score

157. How Do We Create Buy-in?
<--- Score

158. How do senior leaders deploy your organizations vision and values through your leadership system, to the workforce, to key suppliers and partners, and to customers and other stakeholders, as appropriate?
<--- Score

159. Who are the key stakeholders?
<--- Score

160. How do we ensure that implementations of Recruitment Process Outsourcing RPO products are done in a way that ensures safety?
<--- Score

161. What kind of crime could a potential new hire have committed that would not only not disqualify him/her from being hired by our organization, but would actually indicate that he/she might be a particularly good fit?
<--- Score

162. If we do not follow, then how to lead?
<--- Score

163. What is the estimated value of the project?

<--- Score

164. What role does communication play in the success or failure of a Recruitment Process Outsourcing RPO project?
<--- Score

165. How do I stay inspired?
<--- Score

166. How important is Recruitment Process Outsourcing RPO to the user organizations mission?
<--- Score

167. In a project to restructure Recruitment Process Outsourcing RPO outcomes, which stakeholders would you involve?
<--- Score

168. How do we keep the momentum going?
<--- Score

169. What is a feasible sequencing of reform initiatives over time?
<--- Score

170. Instead of going to current contacts for new ideas, what if you reconnected with dormant contacts--the people you used to know? If you were going reactivate a dormant tie, who would it be?
<--- Score

171. How do we provide a safe environment -physically and emotionally?
<--- Score

172. What is Effective Recruitment Process Outsourcing RPO?
<--- Score

173. Do you see more potential in people than they do in themselves?
<--- Score

174. Why should we adopt a Recruitment Process Outsourcing RPO framework?
<--- Score

175. What did we miss in the interview for the worst hire we ever made?
<--- Score

176. Have benefits been optimized with all key stakeholders?
<--- Score

177. To whom do you add value?
<--- Score

178. Marketing budgets are tighter, consumers are more skeptical, and social media has changed forever the way we talk about Recruitment Process Outsourcing RPO. How do we gain traction?
<--- Score

179. What happens when a new employee joins the organization?
<--- Score

180. Do you have an implicit bias for capital investments over people investments?

<--- Score

181. Whose voice (department, ethnic group, women, older workers, etc) might you have missed hearing from in your company, and how might you amplify this voice to create positive momentum for your business?
<--- Score

182. Are the assumptions believable and achievable?
<--- Score

183. How Do We Know if We Are Successful?
<--- Score

184. Who, on the executive team or the board, has spoken to a customer recently?
<--- Score

185. How much contingency will be available in the budget?
<--- Score

186. Where can we break convention?
<--- Score

187. How do we maintain Recruitment Process Outsourcing RPO's Integrity?
<--- Score

188. Do you keep 50% of your time unscheduled?
<--- Score

189. How will we build a 100-year startup?
<--- Score

190. What trophy do we want on our mantle?
<--- Score

191. What would I recommend my friend do if he were facing this dilemma?
<--- Score

192. What is your BATNA (best alternative to a negotiated agreement)?
<--- Score

193. Are we paying enough attention to the partners our company depends on to succeed?
<--- Score

194. Who are you going to put out of business, and why?
<--- Score

195. What are all of our Recruitment Process Outsourcing RPO domains and what do they do?
<--- Score

196. Which models, tools and techniques are necessary?
<--- Score

197. What one word do we want to own in the minds of our customers, employees, and partners?
<--- Score

198. What are the rules and assumptions my industry operates under? What if the opposite were true?
<--- Score

199. If I had to leave my organization for a year and the only communication I could have with employees was a single paragraph, what would I write?
<--- Score

200. How likely is it that a customer would recommend our company to a friend or colleague?
<--- Score

201. Do Recruitment Process Outsourcing RPO rules make a reasonable demand on a users capabilities?
<--- Score

202. If you were responsible for initiating and implementing major changes in your organization, what steps might you take to ensure acceptance of those changes?
<--- Score

203. What do we do when new problems arise?
<--- Score

204. Which individuals, teams or departments will be involved in Recruitment Process Outsourcing RPO?
<--- Score

205. How do we foster innovation?
<--- Score

206. If no one would ever find out about my accomplishments, how would I lead differently?
<--- Score

207. What is the funding source for this project?
<--- Score

208. What potential megatrends could make our business model obsolete?

<--- Score

209. Your reputation and success is your lifeblood, and Recruitment Process Outsourcing RPO shows you how to stay relevant, add value, and win and retain customers

<--- Score

210. Recruitment Process Outsourcing RPO Service Sales Supply Chain, Procurement, Distribution

<--- Score

211. Who uses our product in ways we never expected?

<--- Score

212. What are the basics of Recruitment Process Outsourcing RPO fraud?

<--- Score

213. What have we done to protect our business from competitive encroachment?

<--- Score

214. Who is going to care?

<--- Score

215. Are new benefits received and understood?

<--- Score

216. What knowledge, skills and characteristics mark a good Recruitment Process Outsourcing RPO project manager?

<--- Score

217. Will I get fired?

<--- Score

Add up total points for this section:
_____ = Total points for this section

Divided by: _____ (number of
statements answered) = _____
Average score for this section

Transfer your score to the Recruitment
Process Outsourcing RPO Index at the
beginning of the Self-Assessment.

Recruitment Process Outsourcing RPO and Managing Projects, Criteria for Project Managers:

1.0 Initiating Process Group: Recruitment Process Outsourcing RPO

1. How do you help others satisfy their needs?

2. Are stakeholders properly informed about the status of the Recruitment Process Outsourcing RPO project?

3. Were resources available as planned?

4. How Will You Do It?

5. Who supports, improves, and oversees standardized processes related to the Recruitment Process Outsourcing RPO project's program?

6. At which CMMI level are software processes documented, standardized, and integrated into a standard to-be practiced process for your organization?

7. Have you evaluated the teams performance and asked for feedback?

8. When are the deliverables to be generated in each phase?

9. When will the Recruitment Process Outsourcing RPO project be done?

10. Who is funding the Recruitment Process Outsourcing RPO project?

11. What were the challenges that you encountered

during the execution of a previous Recruitment Process Outsourcing RPO project that you would not want to repeat?

12. Although the Recruitment Process Outsourcing RPO project manager does not directly manage procurement and contracting activities, who does manage procurement and contracting activities in your organization then if not the PM?

13. Are the changes in your Recruitment Process Outsourcing RPO project being formally requested, analyzed, and approved by the appropriate decision makers?

14. What are the required resources?

15. What is the stake of others in your Recruitment Process Outsourcing RPO project?

16. Am I just doing busywork to pass the time?

17. How well did the chosen processes produce the expected results?

18. Does the Recruitment Process Outsourcing RPO project team have enough people to execute the Recruitment Process Outsourcing RPO project plan?

19. Were escalated issues resolved promptly?

20. Which of Six Sigmas DMAIC phases focuses on the measurement of internal process that affect factors that are critical to quality?

1.1 Project Charter: Recruitment Process Outsourcing RPO

21. Why Executive Support?

22. Are there special technology requirements?

23. How high should you set our goals?

24. Will this replace an existing product?

25. Are you building in-house ?

26. Rough time estimate 2 months or 2 yrs?

27. Who is the Recruitment Process Outsourcing RPO project Manager?

28. What are some examples of a business case?

29. What material?

30. Assumptions and Constraints: What assumptions were made in defining Recruitment Process Outsourcing RPO project?

31. Major High-Level Milestone Targets: What events measure progress?

32. Where does all this information come from?

33. Run it as as a startup?

34. Who Manages Integration?

35. What is the purpose of the Recruitment Process Outsourcing RPO project?

36. Customer Benefits: What customer requirements does this Recruitment Process Outsourcing RPO project address?

37. How will you learn more about the process or system youre trying to improve?

38. Why Do you Manage Integration?

39. Is time of the essence?

40. When will this occur?

1.2 Stakeholder Register: Recruitment Process Outsourcing RPO

41. How should employers make their voices heard?

42. Who wants to talk about Security?

43. How Big is the Gap?

44. Who are the stakeholders?

45. What opportunities exist to provide communications?

46. What is the power of the stakeholder?

47. What & Why?

48. How will Reports Be Created?

49. Who is Managing Stakeholder Engagement?

50. How much influence do they have on the Recruitment Process Outsourcing RPO project?

51. What are the major Recruitment Process Outsourcing RPO project milestones requiring communications or providing communications opportunities?

52. Is Your Organization Ready for Change?

1.3 Stakeholder Analysis Matrix: Recruitment Process Outsourcing RPO

53. What is their relationship with the Recruitment Process Outsourcing RPO project?

54. Would it be fair to say that cost is a controlling criteria?

55. Do recommendations include actions to address any differential distribution of impacts?

56. Resource Providers; Who can provide resources to ensure the implementation of the Recruitment Process Outsourcing RPO project?

57. Whats the stakeholder's name, whats their function?

58. What is the range you need to look at?

59. Participatory Approach: How will key stakeholders participate in the Recruitment Process Outsourcing RPO project?

60. Who has the power to influence the outcomes of the work?

61. Who are potential allies and opponents?

62. Cashflow, start-up cash-drain?

63. Identify the stakeholders levels most frequently

used –or at least sought– in your Recruitment Process Outsourcing RPO projects and for which purpose?

64. Are there different rules or organizational models for men and women?

65. Why do you need to manage Recruitment Process Outsourcing RPO project Risk?

66. Are the interests in line with the programme objectives?

67. Are they likely to influence the success or failure of your Recruitment Process Outsourcing RPO project?

68. Economy - home, abroad?

69. How to involve media?

70. Is there a clear description of the scope of practice of the Recruitment Process Outsourcing RPO projects educators?

71. Who is directly responsible for decisions on issues important to the Recruitment Process Outsourcing RPO project?

72. New USPs?

2.0 Planning Process Group: Recruitment Process Outsourcing RPO

73. To what extent have the target population and participants made the activities their own, taking an active role in it?

74. To what extent do the intervention objectives and strategies of the Recruitment Process Outsourcing RPO project respond to the organizations plans?

75. What is a Software Development Life Cycle (SDLC)?

76. If you are late, will anybody notice?

77. Are the follow-up indicators relevant and do they meet the quality needed to measure the outputs and outcomes of the Recruitment Process Outsourcing RPO project?

78. Are work methodologies, financial instruments, etc. shared among departments, organizations and Recruitment Process Outsourcing RPO projects?

79. In what way has the Recruitment Process Outsourcing RPO project come up with innovative measures for problem-solving?

80. Is the duration of the programme sufficient to ensure a cycle that will Recruitment Process Outsourcing RPO project the sustainability of the interventions?

81. Professionals want to know what is expected from them; what are the deliverables?

82. What is involved in Recruitment Process Outsourcing RPO project scope management, and why is good Recruitment Process Outsourcing RPO project scope management so important on information technology Recruitment Process Outsourcing RPO projects?

83. Why do IT Recruitment Process Outsourcing RPO projects fail?

84. Is the Recruitment Process Outsourcing RPO project making progress in helping to achieve the set results?

85. Mitigate. What will you do to minimize the impact should a risk event occur?

86. How can you make your needs known?

87. First of all, should any action be taken?

88. Recruitment Process Outsourcing RPO project Assessment; Why did you do this Recruitment Process Outsourcing RPO project?

89. How are the principles of aid effectiveness (ownership, alignment, management for development results and mutual responsibility) being applied in the Recruitment Process Outsourcing RPO project?

90. How will it affect you?

91. Did the programme design/ implementation strategy adequately address the planning stage necessary to set up structures, hire staff etc.?

2.1 Project Management Plan: Recruitment Process Outsourcing RPO

92. What worked well?

93. Did the planning effort collaborate to develop solutions that integrate expertise, policies, programs, and Recruitment Process Outsourcing RPO projects across entities?

94. What are the training needs?

95. What Went Right?

96. Are comparable cost estimates used for comparing, screening and selecting alternative plans, and has a reasonable cost estimate been developed for the recommended plan?

97. What are the assumptions?

98. Is the budget realistic?

99. What are the assigned resources?

100. Are there non-structural buyout or relocation recommendations?

101. Will you add a schedule and diagram?

102. Who is the sponsor?

103. What does management expect of PMs?

104. What data/reports/tools/etc. do program managers need?

105. What are the deliverables?

106. What goes into your Recruitment Process Outsourcing RPO project Charter?

107. Are calculations and results of analyses essentially correct?

108. If the Recruitment Process Outsourcing RPO project management plan is a comprehensive document that guides you in Recruitment Process Outsourcing RPO project execution and control, then what should it NOT contain?

109. What if, for example, the positive direction and vision of the organization causes expected trends to change resulting in greater need than expected?

2.2 Scope Management Plan: Recruitment Process Outsourcing RPO

110. How do you handle uncertainty or conflict?

111. Describe the process for accepting the Recruitment Process Outsourcing RPO project deliverables. Will the Recruitment Process Outsourcing RPO project deliverables become accepted in writing?

112. Is there an on-going process in place to monitor Recruitment Process Outsourcing RPO project risks?

113. Is quality monitored from the perspective of the customers needs and expectations?

114. Are the quality tools and methods identified in the Quality Plan appropriate to the Recruitment Process Outsourcing RPO project?

115. Are individual tasks of reasonable time effort (8–40 hours)?

116. Are changes in deliverable commitments agreed to by all affected groups & individuals?

117. Has the organization done similar tasks before?

118. Do you keep stake holders informed?

119. Who is responsible for monitoring the Recruitment Process Outsourcing RPO project scope

to ensure the Recruitment Process Outsourcing RPO project remains within the scope baseline?

120. The greatest degree of uncertainty is encountered during which phase of the Recruitment Process Outsourcing RPO project life cycle?

121. How will scope changes be identified and classified?

122. When will scope verification be performed?

123. How do you know when you are finished?

124. Are there any scope changes proposed for the previously authorized Recruitment Process Outsourcing RPO project?

125. Have adequate procedures been put in place for Recruitment Process Outsourcing RPO project communication and status reporting across Recruitment Process Outsourcing RPO project boundaries (for example interdependent software development among interfacing systems)?

126. Are the results of quality assurance reviews provided to affected groups & individuals?

127. Have the procedures for identifying budget variances been followed?

128. Are staffing resource estimates sufficiently detailed and documented for use in planning and tracking the Recruitment Process Outsourcing RPO project?

129. Has process improvement efforts been completed before requirements efforts begin?

2.3 Requirements Management Plan: Recruitment Process Outsourcing RPO

130. Define the Help Desk model. Who will take full responsibility?

131. How often will the reporting occur?

132. Who will approve the requirements (and if multiple approvers, in what order)?

133. Is any organizational data being used or stored?

134. Who is responsible for quantifying the Recruitment Process Outsourcing RPO project requirements?

135. Who has the authority to reject Recruitment Process Outsourcing RPO project requirements?

136. Has the requirements team been instructed in the Change Control process?

137. Is the user satisfied?

138. Controlling Recruitment Process Outsourcing RPO project requirements involves monitoring the status of the Recruitment Process Outsourcing RPO project requirements and managing changes to the requirements. Who is responsible for monitoring and tracking the Recruitment Process Outsourcing RPO project requirements?

139. How knowledgeable is the primary Stakeholder(s) in the proposed application area?

140. Did you distinguish the scope of work the contractor(s) will be required to do?

141. Is there formal agreement on who has authority to request a change in requirements?

142. Who will perform the analysis?

143. Do you know which stakeholders will participate in the requirements effort?

144. How will you develop the schedule of requirements activities?

145. Is Requirements work dependent on any other specific Recruitment Process Outsourcing RPO project or non-Recruitment Process Outsourcing RPO project activities (e.g. funding, approvals, procurement)?

146. Who came up with this requirement?

147. Will you perform a Requirements Risk assessment and develop a plan to deal with risks?

148.   Why Manage Requirements?

149. What Went Wrong?

2.4 Requirements Documentation: Recruitment Process Outsourcing RPO

150. What is a show stopper in the requirements?

151. How will the proposed Recruitment Process Outsourcing RPO project help?

152. What are the attributes of a customer?

153. Verifiability. Can the requirements be checked?

154. What are current process problems?

155. How can you document system requirements?

156. How much testing do you need to do to prove that my system is safe?

157. What Can Tools Do For Us?

158. What if the system wasn t implemented?

159. Are there legal issues?

160. Can the requirement be changed without a large impact on other requirements?

161. How much does requirements engineering cost?

162. What variations exist for a process?

163. How does what is being described meet the

business need?

164. Completeness. Are all functions required by the customer included?

165. How linear / iterative is your Requirements Gathering process (or will it be)?

166. Are all functions required by the customer included?

167. What is your Elevator Speech?

168. What happens when requirements are wrong?

169. Do technical resources exist?

2.5 Requirements Traceability Matrix: Recruitment Process Outsourcing RPO

170. Describe the process for approving requirements so they can be added to the traceability matrix and Recruitment Process Outsourcing RPO project work can be performed. Will the Recruitment Process Outsourcing RPO project requirements become approved in writing?

171. Why use a WBS?

172. How Do you Manage Scope?

173. How small is small enough?

174. Do we have a clear understanding of all subcontracts in place?

175. What are the chronologies, contingencies, consequences, criteria?

176. What is the WBS?

177. What percentage of Recruitment Process Outsourcing RPO projects are producing traceability matrices between requirements and other work products?

178. Is there a requirements traceability process in place?

179. Will you use a Requirements Traceability Matrix?

180. How will it affect the stakeholders personally in their career?

181. Why Do you Manage Scope?

2.6 Project Scope Statement: Recruitment Process Outsourcing RPO

182. Will all tasks resulting from issues be entered into the Recruitment Process Outsourcing RPO project Plan and tracked through the plan?

183. Will tasks be marked complete only after QA has been successfully completed?

184. If there is an independent oversight contractor, have they signed off on the Recruitment Process Outsourcing RPO project Plan?

185. Will the Recruitment Process Outsourcing RPO project risks being managed be according to the Recruitment Process Outsourcing RPO projects risk management process?

186. Name and describe the 2 elements of scope management that deal with concept development ?

187. Did your Recruitment Process Outsourcing RPO project ask for this?

188. Write a brief purpose statement for this Recruitment Process Outsourcing RPO project. Include a business justification statement. What is the product of this Recruitment Process Outsourcing RPO project?

189. Is the quality function identified and assigned?

190. What are some of the major deliverables of the Recruitment Process Outsourcing RPO project?

191. Have you been able to thoroughly document the Recruitment Process Outsourcing RPO projects assumptions and constraints?

192. Is an Issue Management Process documented and filed?

193. Are the input requirements from the team members clearly documented and communicated?

194. Change Management vs. Change Leadership - What's the Difference?

195. Recruitment Process Outsourcing RPO project Lead, Team Lead, Solution Architect?

196. Will an issue form be in use?

197. Will there be documented contingency plans for the top 5-10 risks?

198. How will you verify the accuracy of the work of the Recruitment Process Outsourcing RPO project, and what constitutes acceptance of the deliverables?

199. Are there backup strategies for key members of the Recruitment Process Outsourcing RPO project?

2.7 Assumption and Constraint Log: Recruitment Process Outsourcing RPO

200. Have Recruitment Process Outsourcing RPO project management standards and procedures been established and documented?

201. Are funding and staffing resource estimates sufficiently detailed and documented for use in planning and tracking the Recruitment Process Outsourcing RPO project?

202. Are there nonconformance issues?

203. Has a Recruitment Process Outsourcing RPO project Communications Plan been developed?

204. What do you log?

205. What if failure during recovery?

206. Is the process working, but people are not executing in compliance of the process?

207. Are formal code reviews conducted?

208. Does the Plan conform to standards?

209. Do documented requirements exist for all critical components and areas, including technical, business, interfaces, performance, security and conversion requirements?

210. Are there standards for code development?

211. Can you perform this task or activity in a more effective manner?

212. Is staff trained on the software technologies that are being used on the Recruitment Process Outsourcing RPO project?

213. Are there cosmetic errors that hinder readability and comprehension?

214. Have the scope, objectives, costs, benefits and impacts been communicated to all involved and/or impacted stakeholders and work groups?

215. Does the Recruitment Process Outsourcing RPO project have a formal Recruitment Process Outsourcing RPO project Plan?

216. What is positive about the current process?

217. What Weaknesses do you have?

218. If it is out of compliance, should the process be amended or should the Plan be amended?

219. How do you design an auditing system?

2.8 Work Breakdown Structure: Recruitment Process Outsourcing RPO

220. When do you stop?

221. What is the probability that the Recruitment Process Outsourcing RPO project duration will exceed xx weeks?

222. When does it have to be done?

223. What has to be done?

224. How big is a work-package?

225. Why would you develop a Work Breakdown Structure?

226. How will you and your Recruitment Process Outsourcing RPO project team define the Recruitment Process Outsourcing RPO projects scope and work breakdown structure?

227. Is it still viable?

228. How much detail?

229. Can you make it?

230. Why is it useful?

231. What is the probability of completing the Recruitment Process Outsourcing RPO project in less

that xx days?

232. Do you need another level?

233. How Far Down?

234. Where does it take place?

235. Is it a change in scope?

236. How many levels?

237. Who has to do it?

238. Is the Work breakdown Structure (WBS) defined and is the scope of the Recruitment Process Outsourcing RPO project clear with assigned deliverable owners?

239. When would you develop a Work Breakdown Structure?

2.9 WBS Dictionary: Recruitment Process Outsourcing RPO

240. Is the entire contract planned in time-phased control accounts to the extent practicable?

241. Is authorization of budgets in excess of the contract budget base controlled formally and done with the full knowledge and recognition of the procuring activity?

242. What should you drop in order to add something new?

243. Are records maintained to show how undistributed budgets are controlled?

244. Are all affected work authorizations, budgeting, and scheduling documents amended to properly reflect the effects of authorized changes?

245. Does the sum of all work package budgets plus planning packages within control accounts equal the budgets assigned to those control accounts?

246. Does the contractors system include procedures for measuring the performance of critical subcontractors?

247. Does the contractor require sufficient detailed planning of control accounts to constrain the application of budget initially allocated for future effort to current effort?

248. Major functional areas of contract effort?

249. Are overhead cost budgets established for each organization which has authority to incur overhead costs?

250. Are overhead costs budgets established on a basis consistent with anticipated direct business base?

251. Should you include sub-activities?

252. The WBS is developed as part of a Joint Planning session. But how do you know that youve done this right?

253. Contractor financial periods; for example, annual?

254. Are work packages assigned to performing organizations?

255. Do work packages reflect the actual way in which the work will be done and are they meaningful products or management-oriented subdivisions of a higher level element of work?

256. Changes in the overhead pool and/or organization structures?

257. Are retroactive changes to direct costs and indirect costs prohibited except for the correction of errors and routine accounting adjustments?

258. Is work properly classified as measured effort,

LOE, or apportioned effort and appropriately separated?

259. Does the contractors system provide unit or lot costs when applicable?

2.10 Schedule Management Plan: Recruitment Process Outsourcing RPO

260. Are the key elements of a Recruitment Process Outsourcing RPO project Charter present?

261. Are the constraints or deadlines associated with the task accurate?

262. Is the schedule vertically and horizontally traceable?

263. Have external dependencies been captured in the schedule?

264. Are target dates established for each milestone deliverable?

265. Are all Vendor contracts closed out?

266. Are the schedule estimates reasonable given the Recruitment Process Outsourcing RPO project?

267. Is a payment system in place with proper reviews and approvals?

268. Were Recruitment Process Outsourcing RPO project team members involved in the development of activity & task decomposition?

269. Who is responsible for estimating the activity resources?

270. Are the Recruitment Process Outsourcing RPO project plans updated on a frequent basis?

271. Are metrics used to evaluate and manage Vendors?

272. Define units of measurement for each resource. For example, are you referencing gallons or liters?

273. Is the correct WBS element identified for each task and milestone in the IMS?

274. Is Recruitment Process Outsourcing RPO project status reviewed with the steering and executive teams at appropriate intervals?

275. Recruitment Process Outsourcing RPO project Definition & Scope?

276. Are Vendor invoices audited for accuracy before payment?

277. Are issues raised, assessed, actioned, and resolved in a timely and efficient manner?

278. Have all unresolved risks been documented?

2.11 Activity List: Recruitment Process Outsourcing RPO

279. What went well?

280. What is the least expensive way to complete the Recruitment Process Outsourcing RPO project within 40 weeks?

281. Is there anything planned that doesn t need to be here?

282. In what sequence?

283. For other activities, how much delay can be tolerated?

284. Are the required resources available or need to be acquired?

285. Where will it be performed?

286. What is the total time required to complete the Recruitment Process Outsourcing RPO project if no delays occur?

287. How do you determine the late start (LS) for each activity?

288. When do the individual activities need to start and finish?

289. How difficult will it be to do specific activities on

this Recruitment Process Outsourcing RPO project?

290. When will the work be performed?

291. What will be performed?

292. What is the organization s history in doing similar activities?

293. Is infrastructure setup part of your Recruitment Process Outsourcing RPO project?

294. What are the critical bottleneck activities?

295. Who will perform the work?

296. What is the LF and LS for each activity?

2.12 Activity Attributes: Recruitment Process Outsourcing RPO

297. How Much Activity Detail Is Required?

298. What activity do you think you should spend the most time on?

299. Can more resources be added?

300. Activity: Fair or Not Fair?

301. How many resources do you need to complete the work scope within a limit of X number of days?

302. Has management defined a definite timeframe for the turnaround or Recruitment Process Outsourcing RPO project window?

303. How difficult will it be to do specific activities on this Recruitment Process Outsourcing RPO project?

304. How else could the items be grouped?

305. Where else does it apply?

306. Whats Missing?

307. Were there other ways you could have organized the data to achieve similar results?

308. Whats the general pattern here?

309. Resource is assigned to?

310. Why?

311. Which method produces the more accurate cost assignment?

312. Resources to accomplish the work?

313. How Do you Manage Time?

314. How difficult will it be to complete specific activities on this Recruitment Process Outsourcing RPO project?

2.13 Milestone List: Recruitment Process Outsourcing RPO

315. How late can the activity start?

316. Insurmountable weaknesses?

317. Sustaining internal capabilities?

318. Usps (unique selling points)?

319. Timescales, deadlines and pressures?

320. Political effects?

321. Identify critical paths (one or more) and which activities are on the critical path?

322. What is the market for your technology, product or service?

323. How will you get the word out to customers?

324. How difficult will it be to do specific activities on this Recruitment Process Outsourcing RPO project?

325. Describe the industry you are in and the market growth opportunities. What is the market for your technology, product or service?

326. Own known vulnerabilities?

327. How will the milestone be verified?

328. Do you foresee any technical risks or developmental challenges?

329. How late can each activity be finished and started?

330. Can you derive how soon can the whole Recruitment Process Outsourcing RPO project finish?

331. Sustainable financial backing?

332. How soon can the activity finish?

333. Describe the concept of the technology, product or service that will be or has been developed. How will it be used?

2.14 Network Diagram: Recruitment Process Outsourcing RPO

334. Are the Gantt Chart and/or Network Diagram updated periodically and used to assess the overall Recruitment Process Outsourcing RPO project timetable?

335. Where do you schedule uncertainty time?

336. If X is long, what would be the completion time if you break X into two parallel parts of y weeks and z weeks?

337. What are the tools?

338. Are the required resources available?

339. What activities must occur simultaneously with this activity?

340. What are the Major Administrative Issues?

341. Planning: who, how long, what to do?

342. Exercise: What is the probability that the Recruitment Process Outsourcing RPO project duration will exceed xx weeks?

343. How difficult will it be to do specific activities on this Recruitment Process Outsourcing RPO project?

344. What to do and When?

345. Where Do Schedules Come From?

346. What activity must be completed immediately before this activity can start?

347. What job or jobs could run concurrently?

348. What is the completion time?

349. What job or jobs precede it?

350. If a current contract exists, can you provide the vendor name, contract start, and contract expiration date?

351. Can you calculate the confidence level?

352. If the Recruitment Process Outsourcing RPO project network diagram cannot change but you have extra personnel resources, what is the BEST thing to do?

353. What must be completed before an activity can be started?

2.15 Activity Resource Requirements: Recruitment Process Outsourcing RPO

354. What is the Work Plan Standard?

355. What are constraints that you might find during the Human Resource Planning process?

356. Other support in specific areas?

357. Time for overtime?

358. Anything else?

359. Do you use tools like decomposition and rolling-wave planning to produce the activity list and other outputs?

360. How many signatures do you require on a check and does this match what is in your policy and procedures?

361. When does Monitoring Begin?

362. How do you handle petty cash?

363. Which logical relationship does the PDM use most often?

364. Why do you do that?

365. Are there unresolved issues that need to be addressed?

366. Organizational Applicability?

2.16 Resource Breakdown Structure: Recruitment Process Outsourcing RPO

367. What is the primary purpose of the human resource plan?

368. Why Do you Do It?

369. Changes Based on Input from Stakeholders?

370. Goals for the Recruitment Process Outsourcing RPO project. What is each stakeholders desired outcome for the Recruitment Process Outsourcing RPO project?

371. Which resource planning tool provides information on resource responsibility and accountability?

372. How can this help you with team building?

373. What is each stakeholders desired outcome for the Recruitment Process Outsourcing RPO project?

374. Who delivers the information?

375. Is Predictive Resource Analysis being done?

376. Who will be used as a Recruitment Process Outsourcing RPO project team member?

377. What are the requirements for resource data?

378. Any Changes from Stakeholders?

379. Why Time Management?

380. What s the difference between % Complete and % work?

381. What is the number one predictor of a groups productivity?

382. What Defines a Successful Recruitment Process Outsourcing RPO project?

2.17 Activity Duration Estimates: Recruitment Process Outsourcing RPO

383. Is corrective action taken to bring Recruitment Process Outsourcing RPO project performance into line with the Recruitment Process Outsourcing RPO project plan?

384. Is a contract developed which obligates the seller and the buyer?

385. Do stakeholders follow a procedure for formally accepting the Recruitment Process Outsourcing RPO project scope?

386. What is Earned Value?

387. Which is the BEST Recruitment Process Outsourcing RPO project management tool to use to determine the longest time the Recruitment Process Outsourcing RPO project will take?

388. Does a process exist for approving or rejecting changes?

389. Who will promote it?

390. It under budget or over budget?

391. Are contingency plans created to prepare for risk events to occur?

392. Which is the BEST thing to do to try to complete

a Recruitment Process Outsourcing RPO project two days earlier?

393. Does a process exist to determine the probability of risk events?

394. Are activity dependencies identified?

395. Is action taken to increase the effectiveness and efficiency of Recruitment Process Outsourcing RPO projects?

396. Does a process exist to formally recognize new Recruitment Process Outsourcing RPO projects?

397. Are many products available?

398. Why is there a new or renewed interest in the field of Recruitment Process Outsourcing RPO project management?

399. Do scope statements include the Recruitment Process Outsourcing RPO project objectives and expected deliverables?

400. Did anything besides luck make a difference between success and failure?

401. Is training acquired to enhance the skills, knowledge and capabilities of the Recruitment Process Outsourcing RPO project team?

402. Will the new application negatively affect the current IT infrastructure?

2.18 Duration Estimating Worksheet: Recruitment Process Outsourcing RPO

403. What questions do you have?

404. What utility impacts are there?

405. Small or Large Recruitment Process Outsourcing RPO project?

406. Is a Construction detail attached (to aid in explanation)?

407. Do any colleagues have experience with the company and/or RFPs?

408. What s Next?

409. Does the Recruitment Process Outsourcing RPO project provide innovative ways for Veterans to overcome obstacles or deliver better outcomes?

410. How should ongoing costs be monitored to try to keep the Recruitment Process Outsourcing RPO project within budget?

411. What is your role?

412. What is the total time required to complete the Recruitment Process Outsourcing RPO project if no delays occur?

413. What is the probability the Recruitment Process

Outsourcing RPO project can be completed in 47 weeks?

414. Value Pocket Identification & Quantification What Are Value Pockets?

415. What does it mean to say a task is 75% complete after 3 months?

416. Is the Recruitment Process Outsourcing RPO project responsive to community need?

417. Science = Process: Remember the Scientific Method?

418. Is this operation cost effective?

419. When, then?

2.19 Project Schedule: Recruitment Process Outsourcing RPO

420. What are you counting on?

421. What is Risk?

422. Schedule/Cost Recovery?

423. Are key risk mitigation strategies added to the Recruitment Process Outsourcing RPO project schedule?

424. What is the most mis-scheduled part of process?

425. Did the Recruitment Process Outsourcing RPO project come in on schedule?

426. Understand the constraints used in preparing the schedule. Are activities connected because logic dictates the order in which others occur?

427. Why is this particularly bad?

428. Verify that the update is accurate. Are all remaining durations correct?

429. Have all Recruitment Process Outsourcing RPO project delays been adequately accounted for, communicated to all stakeholders and adjustments made in overall Recruitment Process Outsourcing RPO project schedule?

430. If you can t fix it, how do you do it differently?

431. What is Risk Management?

432. Whats the difference?

433. Are there activities that came from a template or previous Recruitment Process Outsourcing RPO project that are not applicable on this phase of this Recruitment Process Outsourcing RPO project?

434. How do you manage Recruitment Process Outsourcing RPO project Risk?

435. Are you working on the right risks?

436. Your Recruitment Process Outsourcing RPO project management plan results in a Recruitment Process Outsourcing RPO project schedule that is too long. If the Recruitment Process Outsourcing RPO project network diagram cannot change but you have extra personnel resources, what is the BEST thing to do?

437. Was the Recruitment Process Outsourcing RPO project schedule reviewed by all stakeholders and formally accepted?

438. How long does a 12 month Recruitment Process Outsourcing RPO project take?

439. Is there a Schedule Management Plan that establishes the criteria and activities for developing, monitoring and controlling the Recruitment Process Outsourcing RPO project schedule?

2.20 Cost Management Plan: Recruitment Process Outsourcing RPO

440. Alignment to strategic goals & objectives?

441. The definition of the Recruitment Process Outsourcing RPO project scope what needs to be accomplished?

442. Has a Recruitment Process Outsourcing RPO project Communications Plan been developed?

443. Are multiple estimation methods being employed?

444. Planning and scheduling responsibilities – How will the responsibilities for planning and scheduling be allocated?

445. Who should write the PEP?

446. Contracting method – What contracting method is to be used for the contracts?

447. What Is Recruitment Process Outsourcing RPO project Management?

448. Are status reports received per the Recruitment Process Outsourcing RPO project Plan?

449. Has the business need been clearly defined?

450. Best practices implementation – How will change

management be applied to this Recruitment Process Outsourcing RPO project?

451. Scope of work – What is the likelihood and extent of potential future changes to the Recruitment Process Outsourcing RPO project scope?

452. Are actuals compared against estimates to analyze and correct variances?

453. Responsibilities – What is the split of responsibilities between the owner and contractors?

454. Are Recruitment Process Outsourcing RPO project contact logs kept up to date?

455. Are risk oriented checklists used during risk identification?

456. Eac -estimate at completion, what is the total job expected to cost?

457. Are mitigation strategies identified?

458. Is there an onboarding process in place?

459. Was your organizations estimating methodology being used and followed?

2.21 Activity Cost Estimates: Recruitment Process Outsourcing RPO

460. What do you want to know about the stay to know if costs were inappropriately high or low?

461. How difficult will it be to do specific tasks on the Recruitment Process Outsourcing RPO project?

462. What areas does the group agree are the biggest success on the Recruitment Process Outsourcing RPO project?

463. The impact and what actions were taken?

464. Who determines when the contractor is paid?

465. Was it performed on time?

466. Who determines the quality and expertise of contractors?

467. Which contract type places the most risk on the seller?

468. Scope statement only direct or indirect costs as well?

469. How many activities should you have?

470. What were things that you did well, but could improve, and how?

471. What makes a good expected result statement?

472. What is Recruitment Process Outsourcing RPO project Cost Management?

473. Does the activity use a common approach or business function to deliver its results?

474. Was the consultant knowledgeable about the program?

475. Vac -variance at completion, how much over/ under budget do you expect to be?

476. What happens if you cannot produce the documentation for the single audit?

477. Based on your Recruitment Process Outsourcing RPO project communication management plan, what worked well?

478. What cost data should be used to estimate costs during the 2-year follow-up period?

2.22 Cost Estimating Worksheet: Recruitment Process Outsourcing RPO

479. Who is best positioned to know and assist in identifying such factors?

480. What is the purpose of estimating?

481. How will the results be shared and to whom?

482. Ask: are others positioned to know, are others credible, and will others cooperate?

483. Is it feasible to establish a control group arrangement?

484. What Can Be Included?

485. What info is needed?

486. What will others want?

487. Is the Recruitment Process Outsourcing RPO project responsive to community need?

488. Identify the timeframe necessary to monitor progress and collect data to determine how the selected measure has changed?

489. Can a trend be established from historical performance data on the selected measure and are the criteria for using trend analysis or forecasting methods met?

490. What is the estimated labor cost today based upon this information?

491. Does the Recruitment Process Outsourcing RPO project provide innovative ways for stakeholders to overcome obstacles or deliver better outcomes?

492. What happens to any remaining funds not used?

493. What additional Recruitment Process Outsourcing RPO project(s) could be initiated as a result of this Recruitment Process Outsourcing RPO project?

494. What costs are to be estimated?

495. Will the Recruitment Process Outsourcing RPO project collaborate with the local community and leverage resources?

2.23 Cost Baseline: Recruitment Process Outsourcing RPO

496. Are there contingencies or conditions related to the acceptance?

497. Definition of done can be traced back to the definitions of what are you providing to the customer in terms of deliverables?

498. Review your risk triggers -have your risks changed?

499. What is it ?

500. What s the reality?

501. Verify business objectives. Are others appropriate, and well-articulated?

502. What can go wrong?

503. How fast?

504. Is request in line with priorities?

505. What deliverables come first?

506. Has training and knowledge transfer of the operations organization been completed?

507. How will cost estimates be used?

508. What is the organization s history in doing similar tasks?

509. What Threats might prevent us from getting there?

510. What does a good WBS NOT look like?

511. Recruitment Process Outsourcing RPO project Goals -should others be reconsidered?

512. Has operations management formally accepted responsibility for operating and maintaining the product(s) or service(s) delivered by the Recruitment Process Outsourcing RPO project?

2.24 Quality Management Plan: Recruitment Process Outsourcing RPO

513. How do senior leaders review organizational performance?

514. What s the Difference Between a QMP and QAPP?

515. Who is responsible?

516. How do you ensure that your sampling methods and procedures meet your data needs?

517. Where do you focus?

518. No superfluous information or marketing narrative?

519. What is the return on investment?

520. Were there any deficiencies / issues identified in the prior years self-assessment?

521. How are new requirements or changes to requirements identified?

522. Does the program use other agents to collect samples?

523. How is equipment calibrated?

524. How do senior leaders create an organizational focus on customers and other stakeholders?

525. Is this process still needed?

526. What are the established criteria that sampling / testing data are compared against?

527. How are training records kept?

528. How are such standards measured?

529. How do you document and correct nonconformances?

2.25 Quality Metrics: Recruitment Process Outsourcing RPO

530. What approved evidence based screening tools can be used?

531. Which data do others need in one place to target areas of improvement?

532. Were quality attributes reported?

533. Did evaluation start on time?

534. How do you know if everyone is trying to improve the right things?

535. Are there already quality metrics available that detect nonlinear embeddings and trends similar to the users perception?

536. What are the organizations expectations for its quality Recruitment Process Outsourcing RPO project?

537. Has it met internal or external standards?

538. What makes a visualization memorable?

539. When is the security analysis testing complete?

540. Is there alignment within your company on definitions?

541. Product Availability ?

542. Are documents on hand to provide explanations of privacy and confidentiality?

543. Are quality metrics defined?

544. Which report did you use to create the data you are submitting?

545. What metrics do you measure?

546. Is Quality Culture a competitive advantage?

547. Has risk analysis been adequately reviewed?

548. What method of measurement do you use?

2.26 Process Improvement Plan: Recruitment Process Outsourcing RPO

549. What personnel are the coaches for your initiative?

550. Management commitment at all levels?

551. Are you following the quality standards?

552. Why do you want to achieve the goal?

553. What Lessons Have you Learned So Far?

554. Modeling current processes is great, but will you ever see a return on that investment?

555. What personnel are the change agents for your initiative?

556. What personnel are the champions for the initiative?

557. Does our process ensure quality?

558. Everyone agrees on what process improvement is, right?

559. What Is the Test-Cycle Concept?

560. How Do you Manage Quality?

561. Why Quality Management?

562. Have the frequency of collection and the points in the process where measurements will be made been determined?

563. Are you Making Progress on the Goals?

564. Are you Making Progress on the Improvement Framework?

565. What personnel are the sponsors for that initiative?

566. Have the supporting tools been developed or acquired?

567. Where do you want to be?

2.27 Responsibility Assignment Matrix: Recruitment Process Outsourcing RPO

568. Is data disseminated to the contractors management timely, accurate, and usable?

569. Does the Recruitment Process Outsourcing RPO project need to be analyzed further to uncover additional responsibilities?

570. Are material costs reported within the same period as that in which BCWP is earned for that material?

571. What Do You Need to Implement Earned Value Management?

572. Are the bases and rates for allocating costs from each indirect pool consistently applied?

573. Do You Know How Your People are Allocated?

574. What Cost Control Tool Do Many Experts Say is Crucial to Recruitment Process Outsourcing RPO project Management?

575. Most people let you know when others re too busy, but are others really too busy?

576. Identify and isolate causes of favorable and unfavorable cost and schedule variances?

577. Budgets assigned to control accounts?

578. Actual cost of work performed?

579. Are records maintained to show how management reserves are used?

580. What are the constraints?

581. What simple tool can you use to help identify and prioritize Recruitment Process Outsourcing RPO project risks thats very low tech and high touch?

582. If a role has only Signing-off, or only Communicating responsibility and has no Performing, Accountable, or Monitoring responsibility, is it necessary?

583. What can you do to improve productivity?

584. Who is Responsible for Work and Budgets for Each WBS?

585. Changes in the current direct and Recruitment Process Outsourcing RPO projected base?

586. Does the scheduling system identify in a timely manner the status of work?

2.28 Roles and Responsibilities: Recruitment Process Outsourcing RPO

587. Where are you most strong as a supervisor?

588. Required Skills, Knowledge, Experience?

589. Does the team have access to and ability to use data analysis tools?

590. Who is involved?

591. Have you ever been a part of this team?

592. What should you do now to prepare for your career 5+ years from now?

593. Accountabilities: What are the roles and responsibilities of individual team members?

594. Authority: What areas/Recruitment Process Outsourcing RPO projects in your work do you have the authority to decide upon and act on those decisions?

595. Key conclusions and recommendations: Are conclusions and recommendations relevant and acceptable?

596. Is feedback clearly communicated and non-judgmental?

597. Does our vision/mission support a culture of

quality data?

598. Be specific; avoid generalities. Thank you and great work alone are insufficient. What exactly do you appreciate and why?

599. Are our policies supportive of a culture of quality data?

600. Are Recruitment Process Outsourcing RPO project team roles and responsibilities identified and documented?

601. Are the quality assurance functions and related roles and responsibilities clearly defined?

602. To decide whether to use a quality measurement, ask how will I know when it is achieved?

603. Are Recruitment Process Outsourcing RPO project team roles and responsibilities identified and documented?

604. What should you highlight for improvement?

605. What should you do now to ensure that you are meeting all expectations of your current position?

606. Are governance roles and responsibilities documented?

2.29 Human Resource Management Plan: Recruitment Process Outsourcing RPO

607. What talent is needed?

608. Is the Steering Committee active in Recruitment Process Outsourcing RPO project oversight?

609. Are enough systems & user personnel assigned to the Recruitment Process Outsourcing RPO project?

610. Was the scope definition used in task sequencing?

611. Are assumptions being identified, recorded, analyzed, qualified and closed?

612. Is stakeholder involvement adequate?

613. Are tasks tracked by hours?

614. Does all Recruitment Process Outsourcing RPO project documentation reside in a common repository for easy access?

615. Recruitment Process Outsourcing RPO project Objectives?

616. List roles. What commitments have been made?

617. Personnel with expertise?

618. Are quality inspections and review activities listed in the Recruitment Process Outsourcing RPO project schedule(s)?

619. Do you have the reasons why the changes to the organizational systems and capabilities are required?

620. Quality Assurance overheads?

621. Are change requests logged and managed?

622. Are Recruitment Process Outsourcing RPO project contact logs kept up to date?

2.30 Communications Management Plan: Recruitment Process Outsourcing RPO

623. What is the political influence?

624. Can you think of other people who might have concerns or interests?

625. Are you constantly rushing from meeting to meeting?

626. How much time does it take to do it?

627. Who were proponents/opponents?

628. What data is going to be required?

629. Are others part of the communications management plan?

630. Are others needed?

631. Who is involved as you identify stakeholders?

632. What to know?

633. Which stakeholders can influence others?

634. How Did the Term Stakeholder Originate?

635. Who did you turn to if you had questions?

636. Do you prepare stakeholder engagement plans?

637. How were such initiatives successful?

638. What approaches to you feel are the best ones to use?

639. Do you ask; can you recommend others for me to talk with about this initiative?

640. Who to learn from?

641. Who are the members of the governing body?

2.31 Risk Management Plan: Recruitment Process Outsourcing RPO

642. Market risk -Will the new service or product be useful to the organization or marketable to others?

643. How Is The Audit Profession Changing?

644. Should the risk be taken at all?

645. Are requirements fully understood by the software engineering team and customers?

646. What will the damage be?

647. User Involvement: Do I have the right users?

648. What are the cost, schedule and resource impacts if the risk does occur?

649. How would you suggest monitoring for risk transition indicators?

650. Minimize cost and financial risk?

651. Is the process being followed?

652. How much risk protection can you afford?

653. Why do you want risk management?

654. If you cant fix it, how do you do it differently?

655. Are enough people available?

656. Is this an issue, action item, question or a risk?

657. Are certain activities taking a long time to complete?

658. How is Risk Monitoring Performed?

659. Are some people working on multiple Recruitment Process Outsourcing RPO projects?

2.32 Risk Register: Recruitment Process Outsourcing RPO

660. Budget and Schedule: What are the estimated costs and schedules for performing risk-related activities?

661. Who is going to do it?

662. Can the likelihood and impact of failing to achieve such recommendations and action plans be assessed?

663. Is further information required before making a decision?

664. Financial risk -can the organization afford to undertake the Recruitment Process Outsourcing RPO project?

665. When is it going to be done?

666. What risks might negatively or positively affect achieving the Recruitment Process Outsourcing RPO project objectives?

667. Schedule Impact/Severity Estimated Range (workdays) Assume the event happens, what is the potential impact?

668. What may happen or not go according to plan?

669. Having taken action, how did the responses

effect change, and where is the Recruitment Process Outsourcing RPO project now?

670. How could such Risk affect the Recruitment Process Outsourcing RPO project in terms of cost and schedule?

671. What is our current and future risk profile?

672. Does the evidence highlight any areas to advance opportunities or foster good relations. If yes what steps will be taken?

673. How is a Community Risk Register created?

674. Why would you develop a risk register?

675. How are Risks Identified?

676. What further options might be available for responding to the risk?

677. People risk -Are people with appropriate skills available to help complete the Recruitment Process Outsourcing RPO project?

678. Are there any knock-on effects/impact on any of the other areas?

2.33 Probability and Impact Assessment: Recruitment Process Outsourcing RPO

679. Who will be responsible for a slippage?

680. What are the current demands of the customer?

681. Do you have a mechanism for managing change?

682. Are flexibility and reuse paramount?

683. Would avoiding any of such impact the Recruitment Process Outsourcing RPO project's chance of success?

684. Is the number of people on the Recruitment Process Outsourcing RPO project team adequate to do the job?

685. What action do you usually take against risks?

686. Have customers been involved fully in the definition of requirements?

687. What is the likelihood of a breakthrough?

688. What should be the level of difficulty in handling the technology?

689. What is the risk appetite?

690. Are formal technical reviews part of this process?

691. What are the uncertainties associated with the technology selected for the Recruitment Process Outsourcing RPO project?

692. Assumptions Analysis -what assumptions have you made or been given about your Recruitment Process Outsourcing RPO project?

693. How do risks change during the Recruitment Process Outsourcing RPO projects life cycle?

694. Do you have specific methods that you use for each phase of the process?

695. Are staff committed for the duration of the Recruitment Process Outsourcing RPO project?

696. What can you do about it?

697. Which risks need to move on to Perform Quantitative Risk Analysis?

698. Is a software Recruitment Process Outsourcing RPO project management tool available?

2.34 Probability and Impact Matrix: Recruitment Process Outsourcing RPO

699. Is the process supported by tools?

700. Is the Recruitment Process Outsourcing RPO project cutting across the entire organization?

701. Workarounds are determined during which risk management process?

702. Which is an input to the risk management process?

703. What are data sources?

704. Why do you need to manage Recruitment Process Outsourcing RPO project Risk?

705. Who has experience with this?

706. Sensitivity Analysis -Which risks will have the most impact on the Recruitment Process Outsourcing RPO project?

707. What are the probable external agencies to act as Recruitment Process Outsourcing RPO project manager?

708. Do others match with the clients requirement?

709. Is the customer willing to establish rapid communication links with the developer?

710. Can you avoid altogether some things that might go wrong?

711. What is the likely future demand of the customer?

712. During Recruitment Process Outsourcing RPO project executing, a major problem occurs that was not included in the risk register. What should you do FIRST?

713. How do risks change during the Recruitment Process Outsourcing RPO projects life cycle?

714. What is the likelihood?

715. Can you handle the investment risk?

716. Is the number of people on the Recruitment Process Outsourcing RPO project team adequate to do the job?

2.35 Risk Data Sheet: Recruitment Process Outsourcing RPO

717. What was Measured?

718. What is the chance that it will happen?

719. Who has a vested interest in how you perform as an organization (our stakeholders)?

720. Risk of What?

721. Type of Risk Identified?

722. If it happens, what are the consequences?

723. During work activities could hazards exist?

724. Whom do you serve (customers)?

725. How can it happen?

726. What are the main opportunities available to us that you should grab while you can?

727. Are new hazards created?

728. What actions can be taken to eliminate or remove risk?

729. What are you weak at and therefore need to do better?

730. What will be the consequences if it happens?

731. How can hazards be reduced?

732. What are you trying to achieve (Objectives)?

733. Do effective diagnostic tests exist?

734. What is the duration of infection (the length of time the host is infected with the organizm) in a normal healthy human host?

735. What can happen?

736. Will revised controls lead to tolerable risk levels?

2.36 Procurement Management Plan: Recruitment Process Outsourcing RPO

737. Are adequate resources provided for the quality assurance function?

738. Are Recruitment Process Outsourcing RPO project leaders committed to this Recruitment Process Outsourcing RPO project full time?

739. Is Recruitment Process Outsourcing RPO project status reviewed with the steering and executive teams at appropriate intervals?

740. Are risk triggers captured?

741. Are procurement deliverables arriving on time and to specification?

742. Pareto diagrams, statistical sampling, flow charting or trend analysis used quality monitoring?

743. What areas are overlooked on this Recruitment Process Outsourcing RPO project?

744. Are software metrics formally captured, analyzed and used as a basis for other Recruitment Process Outsourcing RPO project estimates?

745. Have the key functions and capabilities been defined and assigned to each release or iteration?

746. Were Recruitment Process Outsourcing RPO

project team members involved in the development of activity & task decomposition?

747. Are cause and effect determined for risks when others occur?

748. Are the Recruitment Process Outsourcing RPO project plans updated on a frequent basis?

749. Has the Recruitment Process Outsourcing RPO project manager been identified?

750. Are Recruitment Process Outsourcing RPO project team members committed fulltime?

751. Is PERT / Critical Path or equivalent methodology being used?

752. Is there a Steering Committee in place?

753. Is there a set of procedures defining the scope, procedures, and deliverables defining quality control?

754. Staffing Requirements?

2.37 Source Selection Criteria: Recruitment Process Outsourcing RPO

755. In the technical/management area, what criteria do you use to determine the final evaluation ratings?

756. What past performance information should be requested?

757. What is cost analysis and when should it be performed?

758. What is the basis of an estimate and what assumptions were made?

759. What is the role of counsel in the procurement process?

760. What should clarifications include?

761. Are types/quantities of material, facilities appropriate?

762. Comparison of each offer's prices to the estimated prices -are there significant differences?

763. How do you ensure an integrated assessment of proposals?

764. Do proposed hours support content and schedule?

765. Have team members been adequately trained?

766. How should the oral presentations be handled?

767. What management structure does the organization consider as optimal for performing the contract?

768. Is This a Cost Contract?

769. Is experience evaluated?

770. In order of importance, which evaluation criteria are the most critical to the determination of your overall rating?

771. What information is to be provided and when should it be provided?

772. What should a DRFP include?

773. How much past performance information should be requested?

2.38 Stakeholder Management Plan: Recruitment Process Outsourcing RPO

774. Are there unnecessary steps that are creating bottlenecks and/or causing people to wait?

775. What is the difference between product and Recruitment Process Outsourcing RPO project scope?

776. Is the quality assurance team identified?

777. What methods are to be used for managing and monitoring subcontractors (eg agreements, contracts etc)?

778. What preventative action can be taken to reduce the likelihood a risk will be realised?

779. What proven methodologies and standards will be used to ensure that materials, products, processes and services are fit for their purpose?

780. Are meeting objectives identified for each meeting?

781. What potential impact does the stakeholder have on the Recruitment Process Outsourcing RPO project?

782. Is there a requirements change management processes in place?

783. Does the Recruitment Process Outsourcing RPO project have a Statement of Work?

784. What are the advantages and disadvantages of using external contracted resources?

785. How are the overall Recruitment Process Outsourcing RPO project development processes to be undertaken to produce the Recruitment Process Outsourcing RPO project outputs?

786. Were Recruitment Process Outsourcing RPO project team members involved in the development of activity & task decomposition?

787. Does this include subcontracted development?

2.39 Change Management Plan: Recruitment Process Outsourcing RPO

788. Are work location changes required?

789. How prevalent is Resistance to Change?

790. Are there any restrictions on who can receive the communications?

791. How many people are required in each of the roles?

792. What are you trying to achieve as a result of communication?

793. Do there need to be new channels developed?

794. What prerequisite knowledge or training is required?

795. What time commitment will this involve?

796. How do you know the requirements you documented are the right ones?

797. What are the key change management success metrics?

798. Do the proposed users have access to the appropriate documentation?

799. What change processes have you experienced in

your organization in the last 2 years?

800. What are the major changes to processes?

801. What new behaviours are required?

802. Is there a support model for this application and are the details available for distribution?

803. Has the relevant business unit been notified of installation and support requirements?

804. Has a training need analysis been carried out?

805. What new competencies will be required for the roles?

3.0 Executing Process Group: Recruitment Process Outsourcing RPO

806. What is the product of your Recruitment Process Outsourcing RPO project?

807. Who are the Recruitment Process Outsourcing RPO project stakeholders?

808. How does a Recruitment Process Outsourcing RPO project life cycle differ from a product life cycle?

809. Are decisions made in a timely manner?

810. Just how important is your work to the overall success of the Recruitment Process Outsourcing RPO project?

811. Could a new application negatively affect the current IT infrastructure?

812. Is the programme supported by national and/or local institutions?

813. What are crucial elements of successful Recruitment Process Outsourcing RPO project plan execution?

814. Will a new application be developed using existing hardware, software, and networks?

815. How will you avoid scope creep?

816. Does the Recruitment Process Outsourcing RPO project team have the right skills?

817. What factors are contributing to progress or delay in the achievement of products and results?

818. Does the case present a realistic scenario?

819. What is the difference between conceptual, application, and evaluative questions?

820. What are deliverables of your Recruitment Process Outsourcing RPO project?

821. What type of information goes in the quality assurance plan?

822. Do your results resemble a normal distribution?

823. How does Recruitment Process Outsourcing RPO project management relate to other disciplines?

824. Does software appear easy to learn?

825. Do Recruitment Process Outsourcing RPO project managers understand the organizational context for their Recruitment Process Outsourcing RPO projects?

3.1 Team Member Status Report: Recruitment Process Outsourcing RPO

826. Are the organization's Recruitment Process Outsourcing RPO projects more successful over time?

827. When a teams productivity and success depend on collaboration and the efficient flow of information, what generally fails them?

828. Is there evidence that staff is taking a more professional approach toward management of the organizations Recruitment Process Outsourcing RPO projects?

829. How it is to be done?

830. Are the products of the organization's Recruitment Process Outsourcing RPO projects meeting their customer's objectives?

831. Do you have an Enterprise Recruitment Process Outsourcing RPO project Management Office (EPMO)?

832. Why is it to be done?

833. The problem with Reward & Recognition Programs is that the truly deserving people all too often get left out. How can you make it practical?

834. Will the staff do training or is that done by a third party?

835. How can you make it practical?

836. What specific interest groups do you have in place?

837. What is to be done?

838. Does the product, good, or service already exist within the organization?

839. How will Resource Planning be done?

840. How does this product, good, or service meet the needs of the Recruitment Process Outsourcing RPO project and the organization as a whole?

841. Does the organization have the means (staff, money, contract, etc.) to produce or to acquire the product, good, or service?

842. Does every department have to have a Recruitment Process Outsourcing RPO project Manager on staff?

843. How much risk is involved?

844. Are the attitudes of staff regarding Recruitment Process Outsourcing RPO project work improving?

3.2 Change Request: Recruitment Process Outsourcing RPO

845. What should be regulated in a change control operating instruction?

846. How well do experienced software developers predict software change?

847. Who Will Perform the Change?

848. What kind of information about the change request needs to be captured?

849. Will this change conflict with other requirements changes (e.g., lead to conflicting operational scenarios)?

850. What are the Impacts to an organization?

851. Has a formal technical review been conducted to assess technical correctness?

852. What must be taken into consideration when introducing change control programs?

853. Will new change requests be acknowledged in a timely manner?

854. Customer Acceptance Plan How will the customer verify the change has been implemented successfully?

855. Who is communicating the change?

856. What is a Change Request Form?

857. Are there requirements attributes that are strongly related to the complexity and size?

858. Who needs to approve change requests?

859. How can changes be graded?

860. What mechanism is used to appraise others of changes that are made?

861. How are changes graded and who is responsible for the rating?

862. Will all change requests be unconditionally tracked through this process?

863. Is it feasible to use requirements attributes as predictors of reliability?

3.3 Change Log: Recruitment Process Outsourcing RPO

864. Is the submitted change a new change or a modification of a previously approved change?

865. How does this change affect scope?

866. Do the described changes impact on the integrity or security of the system?

867. Is this a mandatory replacement?

868. How does this change affect the timeline of the schedule?

869. Who initiated the change request?

870. When was the request approved?

871. Should a more thorough impact analysis be conducted?

872. Is the change request open, closed or pending?

873. When was the request submitted?

874. Is the requested change request a result of changes in other Recruitment Process Outsourcing RPO project(s)?

875. Is the change backward compatible without limitations?

876. Does the suggested change request represent a desired enhancement to the products functionality?

877. Will the Recruitment Process Outsourcing RPO project fail if the change request is not executed?

878. Does the suggested change request seem to represent a necessary enhancement to the product?

879. Where Do Changes Come From?

880. Is the change request within Recruitment Process Outsourcing RPO project scope?

881. How does this relate to the standards developed for specific business processes?

3.4 Decision Log: Recruitment Process Outsourcing RPO

882. What is your overall strategy for quality control / quality assurance procedures?

883. Does anything need to be adjusted?

884. How do you know when you are achieving it?

885. Adversarial Environment. Is your opponent open to a non-traditional workflow, or will it likely challenge anything you do?

886. How do you define success?

887. So, what is the line where eDiscovery ends and document review begins?

888. How consolidated and comprehensive a story can we tell by capturing currently available incident data in a central location and through a log of key decisions during an incident?

889. Decision-making process; how will the team make decisions?

890. What eDiscovery problem or issue did your company set out to fix or make better?

891. Is everything working as expected?

892. Linked to original objective?

893. How effective is maintaining the log at facilitating organizational learning?

894. It becomes critical to track and periodically revisit both operational effectiveness; Are you noticing all that you need to, and are you interpreting what you see effectively?

895. How does an increasing emphasis on cost containment influence the strategies and tactics used?

896. Meeting purpose; why does this team meet?

897. Which variables make a critical difference?

898. Who is the decisionmaker?

899. What was the rationale for the decision?

900. What makes you different or better than others companies selling the same thing?

901. Behaviors; what are guidelines that the team has identified that will assist them with getting the most out of their team meetings?

3.5 Quality Audit: Recruitment Process Outsourcing RPO

902. Have personnel cleanliness and health requirements been established?

903. Is the process of self review, learning and improvement endemic throughout the organization?

904. How does the organization know that its relationship with its (past) staff is appropriately effective and constructive?

905. What does an analysis of the organizations staff profile suggest in terms of its planning, and how is this being addressed?

906. How does the organization know that its quality of teaching is appropriately effective and constructive?

907. How does the organization know that its planning processes are appropriately effective and constructive?

908. How does the organization know that its advisory services are appropriately effective and constructive?

909. Are all employees including salespersons made aware that they must report all complaints received from any source for inclusion in the complaint handling system?

910. Are all complaints involving the possible failure of a device, labeling, or packaging to meet any of its specifications reviewed, evaluated, and investigated?

911. Are there sufficient personnel having the necessary education, background, training, and experience to assure that all operations are correctly performed?

912. How are you auditing the organizations compliance with regulations?

913. How do staff know if they are doing a good job?

914. How does the organization know that its system for inducting new staff to maximize their workplace contributions are appropriately effective and constructive?

915. Do the suppliers use a formal quality system?

916. Do the acceptance procedures and specifications include the criteria for acceptance/rejection, define the process to be used, and specify the measuring and test equipment that is to be used?

917. If the organization thinks it is doing something well, can it prove this?

918. Are people allowed to contribute ideas?

919. How does the organization know that its systems for meeting staff extracurricular learning support requirements are appropriately effective and constructive?

920. How does the organization know that its system for ensuring a positive organizational climate is appropriately effective and constructive?

921. How does the organization know that the range and quality of its social and recreational services and facilities are appropriately effective and constructive in meeting the needs of staff?

3.6 Team Directory: Recruitment Process Outsourcing RPO

922. How and in what format should information be presented?

923. Who will write the meeting minutes and distribute?

924. Process Decisions: Are all issues being addressed to the satisfaction of both parties within approximately 30 days from the time the issue is identified?

925. What are you going to deliver or accomplish?

926. How will you accomplish and manage the objectives?

927. Who will be the stakeholders on your next Recruitment Process Outsourcing RPO project?

928. Who will report Recruitment Process Outsourcing RPO project status to all stakeholders?

929. Is construction on schedule?

930. Who will talk to the customer?

931. Where should the information be distributed?

932. Have you decided when to celebrate the Recruitment Process Outsourcing RPO projects

completion date?

933. Process Decisions: Are contractors adequately prosecuting the work?

934. Process Decisions: Do job conditions warrant additional actions to collect job information and document on-site activity?

935. What needs to be communicated?

936. Process Decisions: How well was task order work performed?

937. Who are the Team Members?

938. Decisions: What could be done better to improve the quality of the constructed product?

939. How does the team resolve conflicts and ensure tasks are completed?

3.7 Team Operating Agreement: Recruitment Process Outsourcing RPO

940. Does your team need access to all documents and information at all times?

941. What are the safety issues/risks that need to be addressed and/or that the team needs to discuss?

942. Are there differences in access to communication and collaboration technology based on team member location?

943. What administrative supports will be put in place to support the team and the teams supervisor?

944. Do you leverage technology engagement tools group chat, polls, screen sharing, etc.?

945. Why does the organization want to participate in teaming?

946. Did you determine the technology methods that best match the messages to be communicated?

947. What is Group Supervision?

948. Do you upload presentation materials in advance and test the technology?

949. Are there influences outside the team that may affect performance, and if so, have you identified and addressed them?

950. What is the anticipated procedure (recruitment, solicitation of volunteers, or assignment) for selecting team members?

951. Is compensation based on team and individual performance?

952. Did you prepare participants for the next meeting?

953. Do you vary your voice pace, tone and pitch to engage participants and gain involvement?

954. Do you post meeting notes and the recording (if used) and notify participants?

955. The method to be used in the decision making process; Will it be consensus, majority rule, or the supervisor having the final say?

956. Methodologies: How will key team processes be implemented, such as training, research, work deliverable production, review and approval processes, knowledge management, and meeting procedures?

957. What are the boundaries (organizational or geographic) within which you operate?

958. Must your team members rely on the expertise of other members to complete tasks?

959. Conflict Resolution: How will disputes and other conflicts be mediated or resolved?

3.8 Team Performance Assessment: Recruitment Process Outsourcing RPO

960. To what degree are the skill areas critical to team performance present?

961. To what degree do members articulate the goals beyond the team membership?

962. To what degree will the team adopt a concrete, clearly understood, and agreed-upon approach that will result in achievement of the teams goals?

963. To what degree does the teams purpose contain themes that are particularly meaningful and memorable?

964. To what degree do members understand and articulate the same purpose without relying on ambiguous abstractions?

965. To what degree does the teams approach to its work allow for modification and improvement over time?

966. Do friends perform better than acquaintances?

967. Individual task proficiency and team process behavior: Whats important for team functioning?

968. To what degree can the team ensure that all members are individually and jointly accountable for the teams purpose, goals, approach, and work-

products?

969. If you have received criticism from reviewers that your work suffered from method variance, what was the circumstance?

970. To what degree does the teams work approach provide opportunity for members to engage in fact-based problem solving?

971. To what degree are sub-teams possible or necessary?

972. To what degree will team members, individually and collectively, commit time to help themselves and others learn and develop skills?

973. Does more radicalness mean more perceived benefits?

974. What is method variance?

975. To what degree are the goals ambitious?

976. To what degree can all members engage in open and interactive discussions?

977. When does the medium matter?

978. What are Teams?

979. To what degree does the teams work approach provide opportunity for members to engage in results-based evaluation?

3.9 Team Member Performance Assessment: Recruitment Process Outsourcing RPO

980. How do you work together to improve teaching and learning?

981. How do you make use of research?

982. New skills/knowledge gained this year?

983. How do you currently use the time that is available?

984. To what degree will new and supplemental skills be introduced as the need is recognized?

985. Are the goals SMART ?

986. Are any governance changes sufficient to impact achievement?

987. How do you start collaborating?

988. Do the goals support the organizations goals?

989. How do you determine which data are the most important to use, analyze, or review?

990. What are best practices for delivering and developing training evaluations to maximize the benefits of leveraging emerging technologies?

991. How does your team work together?

992. Who they are?

993. Should a Ratee get a copy of all the Raters documents about the employees performance?

994. What upcoming plans do you have to complete training and assessment Recruitment Process Outsourcing RPO projects (or modify existing Recruitment Process Outsourcing RPO projects) in the next 3 months?

995. Can your organization rate by exception and assume that most employees are performing at an acceptable level?

996. How effective is training that is delivered through technology-based platforms?

997. Did training work?

998. What are Best Practices in use for the Performance Measurement System?

3.10 Issue Log: Recruitment Process Outsourcing RPO

999. In your work, how much time is spent on stakeholder identification?

1000. What is the impact on the Business Case?

1001. Why Multiple Evaluators?

1002. Why not more evaluators?

1003. Who is the stakeholder?

1004. Do you often overlook a key stakeholder or stakeholder group?

1005. Is the Issue Log kept in a safe place?

1006. Are there potential barriers between the team and the stakeholder?

1007. Who reported the issue?

1008. Are the Recruitment Process Outsourcing RPO project Issues uniquely identified, including to which product they refer?

1009. What are the stakeholders interrelationships?

1010. Do you have members of your team responsible for certain stakeholders?

1011. What is the stakeholders political influence?

1012. How do you reply to this question; I am new here and managing this major program. How do you suggest I build my network?

1013. What is the impact on the risks?

1014. Who do you turn to if you have questions?

1015. Why Do you Manage Human Resources?

1016. What is a change?

1017. What is the stakeholders level of authority?

4.0 Monitoring and Controlling Process Group: Recruitment Process Outsourcing RPO

1018. Do clients benefit (change) from the services?

1019. Are the necessary foundations in place to ensure the sustainability of the results of the programme?

1020. How will staff learn how to use the deliverables?

1021. Have operating capacities been created and/or reinforced in partners?

1022. How is Agile Recruitment Process Outsourcing RPO project Management Done?

1023. How many more potential communications channels were introduced by the discovery of the new stakeholders?

1024. Are the services being delivered?

1025. Propriety: Who needs to be involved in the evaluation to be ethical?

1026. Feasibility: How much money, time, and effort can you put into this?

1027. Is there sufficient funding available for this?

1028. What areas does the group agree are the

biggest success on the Recruitment Process Outsourcing RPO project?

1029. What were things that you need to improve?

1030. Is the verbiage used appropriate and understandable?

1031. In what way has the programme come up with innovative measures for problem-solving?

1032. Just how important is your work to the overall success of the Recruitment Process Outsourcing RPO project?

1033. What communication items need improvement?

1034. Accuracy: What design will lead to accurate information?

4.1 Project Performance Report: Recruitment Process Outsourcing RPO

1035. To what degree are the members clear on what they are individually responsible for and what they are jointly responsible for?

1036. To what degree does the team's purpose contain themes that are particularly meaningful and memorable?

1037. What is the PRS?

1038. To what degree can team members vigorously define the team's purpose in discussions with others who are not part of the functioning team?

1039.   To what degree can the cognitive capacity of individuals accommodate the flow of information?

1040. To what degree is the information network consistent with the structure of the formal organization?

1041. To what degree are the goals realistic?

1042. To what degree do team members articulate the team's work approach?

1043. To what degree will each member have the opportunity to advance his or her professional skills in all three of the above categories while contributing to the accomplishment of the team's purpose and goals?

1044. How is the data used?

1045. To what degree are the demands of the task compatible with and converge with the relationships of the informal organization?

1046. To what degree are the demands of the task compatible with and converge with the mission and functions of the formal organization?

1047. What degree are the relative importance and priority of the goals clear to all team members?

1048. To what degree does the task meet individual needs?

1049. To what degree does the team's work approach provide opportunity for members to engage in results-based evaluation?

4.2 Variance Analysis: Recruitment Process Outsourcing RPO

1050. What is the total budget for the Recruitment Process Outsourcing RPO project (including estimates for authorized but unpriced work)?

1051. Are all authorized tasks assigned to identified organizational elements?

1052. Does the accounting system provide a basis for auditing records of direct costs chargeable to the contract?

1053. Can the relationship with problem customers be restructured so that there is a win-win situation?

1054. Are the actual costs used for variance analysis reconcilable with data from the accounting system?

1055. What causes selling price variance?

1056. Historical experience?

1057. Are there quarterly budgets with quarterly performance comparisons?

1058. Is there a logical explanation for any variance?

1059. What is the expected future profitability of each customer?

1060. What should management do?

1061. Are procedures for variance analysis documented and consistently applied at the control account level and selected WBS and organizational levels at least monthly as a routine task?

1062. Are data elements reconcilable between internal summary reports and reports forwarded to the stakeholders?

1063. Other relevant issues of Variance Analysis -selling price or gross margin?

1064. Are there externalities from having some customers, even if they are unprofitable in the short run?

1065. Is the anticipated (firm and potential) business base Recruitment Process Outsourcing RPO projected in a rational, consistent manner?

1066. What does an unfavorable overhead volume variance mean?

1067. Are meaningful indicators identified for use in measuring the status of cost and schedule performance?

4.3 Earned Value Status: Recruitment Process Outsourcing RPO

1068. Earned Value can be used in almost any Recruitment Process Outsourcing RPO project situation and in almost any Recruitment Process Outsourcing RPO project environment. It may be used on large Recruitment Process Outsourcing RPO projects, medium sized Recruitment Process Outsourcing RPO projects, tiny Recruitment Process Outsourcing RPO projects (in cut-down form), complex and simple Recruitment Process Outsourcing RPO projects and in any market sector. Some people, of course, know all about earned value, they have used it for years - but perhaps not as effectively as they could have?

1069. What is the unit of forecast value?

1070. When is it going to finish?

1071. Verification is a process of ensuring that the developed system satisfies the stakeholders agreements and specifications; Are you building the product right? What do you verify?

1072. Validation is a process of ensuring that the developed system will actually achieve the stakeholders desired outcomes; Are you building the right product? What do you validate?

1073. Are you hitting your Recruitment Process Outsourcing RPO projects targets?

1074. Where is Evidence-based Earned Value in your organization reported?

1075. Where are your problem areas?

1076. If earned value management (EVM) is so good in determining the true status of a Recruitment Process Outsourcing RPO project and Recruitment Process Outsourcing RPO project its completion, why is it that hardly any one uses it in information systems related Recruitment Process Outsourcing RPO projects?

1077. How much is it going to cost by the finish?

1078. How does this compare with other Recruitment Process Outsourcing RPO projects?

4.4 Risk Audit: Recruitment Process Outsourcing RPO

1079. What are the costs associated with late delivery or a defective product?

1080. Does the organization have or has considered the need for the following insurance covers: public liability, professional indemnity and directors and officers liability?

1081. Have risks been discussed with an insurance broker or provider and suitable insurance cover been arranged?

1082. Has everyone (staff, volunteers and participants) agreed to a code of behaviour or conduct?

1083. Do you have a consistent repeatable process that is actually used?

1084. What is the implication of budget constraint on this process?

1085. How can the strategy fail/achieved?

1086. What are the risks that could stop us from achieving our objectives?

1087. What expertise does the Board have on quality, outcomes, and errors?

1088. Are all programs planned and conducted

according to recognised safety standards?

1089. Is the customer willing to participate in reviews?

1090. What is the anticipated volatility of the requirements?

1091. Are tools for analysis and design available?

1092. Are procedures in place to ensure the security of staff and information and compliance with privacy legislation if applicable?

1093. Does your organization have a process for meeting its ongoing taxation obligations?

1094. Is the technology to be built new to your organization?

1095. How risk averse are you?

1096. Is there a screening process that will ensure all participants have the fitness and skills required to safely participate?

1097. Does your organization meet the terms of any contracts with which it is involved?

1098. What responsibilities for quality, errors, and outcomes have been delegated to staff (or others) without adequate oversight?

4.5 Contractor Status Report: Recruitment Process Outsourcing RPO

1099. What was the overall budget or estimated cost?

1100. What process manages the contracts?

1101. What is the average response time for answering a support call?

1102. Are there contractual transfer concerns?

1103. Who can list a Recruitment Process Outsourcing RPO project as company experience, the company or a previous employee of the company?

1104. How does the proposed individual meet each requirement?

1105. What was the final actual cost?

1106. If applicable; describe your standard schedule for new software version releases. Are new software version releases included in the standard maintenance plan?

1107. What was the budget or estimated cost for your companys services?

1108. How is Risk Transferred?

1109. How long have you been using the services?

1110. What was the actual budget or estimated cost for your companys services?

1111. Describe how often regular updates are made to the proposed solution. Are these regular updates included in the standard maintenance plan?

1112. What are the minimum and optimal bandwidth requirements for the proposed soluiton?

4.6 Formal Acceptance: Recruitment Process Outsourcing RPO

1113. Does it do what client said it would?

1114. Does it do what Recruitment Process Outsourcing RPO project team said it would?

1115. Was the Recruitment Process Outsourcing RPO project managed well?

1116. Is formal acceptance of the Recruitment Process Outsourcing RPO project product documented and distributed?

1117. Who supplies data?

1118. Was the client satisfied with the Recruitment Process Outsourcing RPO project results?

1119. What features, practices, and processes proved to be strengths or weaknesses?

1120. Was business value realized?

1121. Did the Recruitment Process Outsourcing RPO project manager and team act in a professional and ethical manner?

1122. Was the sponsor/customer satisfied?

1123. Did the Recruitment Process Outsourcing RPO project achieve its MOV?

1124. Was the Recruitment Process Outsourcing RPO project goal achieved?

1125. What can you do better next time?

1126. Was the Recruitment Process Outsourcing RPO project work done on time, within budget, and according to specification?

1127. General estimate of the costs and times to complete the Recruitment Process Outsourcing RPO project?

1128. Do you buy pre-configured systems or build your own configuration?

1129. Do you buy-in installation services?

1130. How well did the team follow the methodology?

1131. How does your team plan to obtain formal acceptance on your Recruitment Process Outsourcing RPO project?

1132. What was done right?

5.0 Closing Process Group: Recruitment Process Outsourcing RPO

1133. What areas were overlooked on this Recruitment Process Outsourcing RPO project?

1134. What is an Encumbrance?

1135. Is there a clear cause and effect between the activity and the lesson learned?

1136. What is the Recruitment Process Outsourcing RPO project name and date of completion?

1137. Were decisions made in a timely manner?

1138. Who are the Recruitment Process Outsourcing RPO project stakeholders?

1139. What was learned?

1140. Will the Recruitment Process Outsourcing RPO project deliverable(s) replace a current asset or group of assets?

1141. If a risk event occurs, what will you do?

1142. What is the overall risk of the Recruitment Process Outsourcing RPO project to the organization?

1143. How critical is the Recruitment Process Outsourcing RPO project success to the success of the organization?

1144. Were cost budgets met?

1145. Did you do what you said you were going to do?

1146. What were things that you did very well and want to do the same again on the next Recruitment Process Outsourcing RPO project?

1147. Did the delivered product meet the specified requirements and goals of the Recruitment Process Outsourcing RPO project?

1148. What could have been improved?

1149. What is the amount of funding and what Recruitment Process Outsourcing RPO project phases are funded?

1150. If action is called for, what form should it take?

1151. What will you do to minimize the impact should a risk event occur?

5.1 Procurement Audit: Recruitment Process Outsourcing RPO

1152. Was the overall procurement done within a reasonable time?

1153. Has it been determined which areas of procurement the audit should cover?

1154. Is there no evidence of any external or superior pressure to reach a specific result?

1155. Have guidelines been set up for how the procurement process should be conducted?

1156. Were additional deliveries a partial replacement for normal supplies or installations or an extension of existing supplies or installations?

1157. How do you address the risk of fraud and corruption?

1158. Is there a policy on making purchases locally where possible?

1159. Were all admitted tenderers invited to submit a tender for each specific contract?

1160. Are behaviour modification applied to change procurement of goods and services if procurement is not functioning properly?

1161. Was the submission of variant tenders accepted

and duly ruled?

1162. Are lease-purchase agreements drawn and processed in accordance with law and regulation?

1163. In the set up of the system and in the award of contracts were only electronic means used?

1164. Are controls proportionated to risks?

1165. Is the procurement process organized the most appropriate way taking into consideration the amount of procurement?

1166. Is there no evidence of collusion between bidders?

1167. Are advance payments to employees properly authorized and controlled?

1168. Was confidentiality ensured when necessary?

1169. Are approvals needed if changes are made in the quantity or specification of the original purchase requisition?

1170. Did the bidder comply with requests within the deadline set?

1171. Is an appropriated degree of standardization of goods and services respected?

5.2 Contract Close-Out: Recruitment Process Outsourcing RPO

1172. Was the contract sufficiently clear so as not to result in numerous disputes and misunderstandings?

1173. What happens to the recipient of services?

1174. Parties: Authorized?

1175. Was the contract complete without requiring numerous changes and revisions?

1176. A change in knowledge?

1177. A change in attitude or behavior?

1178. Have all contracts been completed?

1179. Have all acceptance criteria been met prior to final payment to contractors?

1180. A change in circumstances?

1181. How is the contracting office notified of the automatic contract close-out?

1182. What is Capture Management?

1183. How/When Used ?

1184. Was the contract type appropriate?

1185. Are the signers the authorized officials?

1186. How does it work?

1187. Have all contract records been included in the Recruitment Process Outsourcing RPO project archives?

1188. Why Outsource?

1189. Has each contract been audited to verify acceptance and delivery?

1190. Have all contracts been closed?

1191. Parties: Who is Involved?

5.3 Project or Phase Close-Out: Recruitment Process Outsourcing RPO

1192. What were the desired outcomes?

1193. What Security Considerations needed to be addressed during the Procurement Life Cycle?

1194. What were the actual outcomes?

1195. What was the preferred delivery mechanism?

1196. If you were the Recruitment Process Outsourcing RPO project sponsor, how would you determine which Recruitment Process Outsourcing RPO project team(s) and/or individuals deserve recognition?

1197. What process was planned for managing issues/ risks?

1198. What is a Risk Management Process?

1199. What benefits or impacts does the stakeholder group expect to obtain as a result of the Recruitment Process Outsourcing RPO project?

1200. How often did each stakeholder need an update?

1201. In preparing the Lessons Learned report, should it reflect a consensus viewpoint, or should the report reflect the different individual viewpoints?

1202. How much influence did the stakeholder have over others?

1203. What hierarchical authority does the stakeholder have in the organization?

1204. Who exerted influence that has positively affected or negatively impacted the Recruitment Process Outsourcing RPO project?

1205. What is in it for you?

1206. Have business partners been involved extensively, and what data was required for them?

1207. What are the mandatory communication needs for each stakeholder?

1208. Who controlled the resources for the Recruitment Process Outsourcing RPO project?

5.4 Lessons Learned: Recruitment Process Outsourcing RPO

1209. Is there any way in which you think our development process hampered this Recruitment Process Outsourcing RPO project?

1210. Does the lesson educate others to improve performance?

1211. Was the necessary hardware, software, accommodation etc available?

1212. How was the political and social history changed over the life of the Recruitment Process Outsourcing RPO project?

1213. To what extent was the evolution of risks communicated?

1214. Under what legal authority did the organization head and program manager direct the organization and Recruitment Process Outsourcing RPO project?

1215. How satisfied are you with your involvement in the development and/or review of the Recruitment Process Outsourcing RPO project Scope during Recruitment Process Outsourcing RPO project Initiation and Planning?

1216. How effective was the architecture/system design process?

1217. Who Needs to Learn Lessons?

1218. Did the delivered product meet the specified requirements and goals of the Recruitment Process Outsourcing RPO project?

1219. How effective were Recruitment Process Outsourcing RPO project audits?

1220. How to Write Up the Lesson Identified – How will you document the results of your analysis such that you have an LI ready to take the next step in the LL process?

1221. How useful was your testing?

1222. How accurately and timely was the Risk Management Log updated or reviewed?

1223. Were the Recruitment Process Outsourcing RPO project Objectives met (If not, briefly explain what wasnt met)?

1224. What things mattered the most on this Recruitment Process Outsourcing RPO project?

1225. How effective was the documentation that you received with the Recruitment Process Outsourcing RPO project product/service?

1226. Was the user/client satisfied with the end product?

1227. How useful was the content of the training you received in preparation for the use of the product/service?

1228. What on the Recruitment Process Outsourcing RPO project worked well and was effective in the delivery of the product?

Index

ability 26, 68, 174
abroad   114
acceptable   43, 59, 174, 218
acceptance   7, 104, 130, 164, 202, 209, 233-234, 239-240
accepted   91, 120, 157, 165, 237
accepting   120, 152
access 2, 9-10, 40, 45, 174, 176, 196, 213
accomplish   8, 64, 85, 143, 211
accordance   238
according   32, 34, 129, 182, 230, 234
account   11, 28, 226
accounted   47, 156
accounting   136, 225
accounts   135, 173
accuracy   48, 130, 139, 222
accurate   10, 96, 138, 143, 156, 172, 222
accurately   244
achievable   102
achieve   8, 56, 60, 63, 85, 116, 142, 170, 182, 189, 196, 227,
233
achieved   17, 61, 85, 175, 229, 234
achieving   182, 206, 229
acquire   201
acquired   140, 153, 171
across 43, 76, 118, 121, 186
action 74, 76, 116, 152-153, 181-182, 184, 194, 236
actionable   37
actioned   139
actions 18, 74, 90, 113, 160, 188, 212
active 115, 176
activities   23, 59, 73, 109, 115, 124, 140-144, 146, 156-157,
160, 177, 181-182, 188
activity 4, 27, 29, 132, 135, 138, 140-142, 144-148, 152-153, 160-
161, 191, 195, 212, 235
actual 29, 136, 173, 225, 231-232, 241
actually   31, 65, 74, 99, 227, 229
actuals 159
addition   9, 91
additional   24, 51, 55, 163, 172, 212, 237
additions   79

address   19, 59, 111, 113, 117, 237
addressed   148, 208, 211, 213, 241
addressing   26, 93
adequate   121, 176, 184, 187, 190, 230
adequately   24, 44, 117, 156, 169, 192, 212
adjusted   206
admitted   237
advance   183, 213, 223, 238
advantage   56, 84, 169
advantages   84, 195
advise 9
advisory   208
affect 52-53, 55, 94, 109, 116, 128, 153, 182-183, 198, 204, 213
affected   120-121, 135, 242
affecting   13, 19, 54
afford   180, 182
against32, 70, 72, 159, 167, 184
agencies   89, 186
agendas   90
agents 166, 170
Aggregate   43
agreed   41-42, 120, 229
Agreement   6, 103, 124, 213
agreements   194, 227, 238
agrees 95, 170
aiming 85
alerts   73
aligned   21
alignment   116, 158, 168
alleged   1
allies   113
allocate   87
allocated   98, 135, 158, 172
allocating   172
allowed   86, 209
allows   10
almost 227
already   88, 168, 201
Although   109
altogether   187
always 10
Amazon   11
ambiguous   215

ambitious   216
amended   132, 135
America   26
amount   236, 238
amplify 50, 102
analyses   119
analysis   3, 7, 12, 38-39, 41-47, 50-54, 56, 63, 65-66, 69, 113,
124, 150, 162, 168-169, 174, 185-186, 190, 192, 197, 204, 208, 225-
226, 230, 244
analyze   2, 41-43, 46, 48-49, 51-52, 64, 159, 217
analyzed   41-42, 44-45, 47, 59, 73, 109, 172, 176, 190
annual 136
another   11, 97, 134
answer 12-13, 17, 24, 36, 49, 58, 70, 81
answered   23, 34, 48, 57, 69, 80, 106
answering   12, 231
anybody   115
anyone   29, 93, 96
anything   140, 148, 153, 206
appear   1, 199
appetite   184
applicable   13, 137, 157, 230-231
applied   76, 116, 159, 172, 226, 237
appointed   28-29
appraise   203
appreciate   175
approach   41, 84, 113, 161, 200, 215-216, 223-224
approaches   64-65, 179
approval   25, 93, 214
approvals   124, 138, 238
approve   123, 203
approved   109, 127, 168, 204
approvers   123
approving   127, 152
Architect   130
Architects   8
archives   240
around 97
arranged   229
arriving 190
articulate   215, 223
asking   1, 8
assess   18, 146, 202

assessed   139, 182
assessing   60, 73
Assessment   5-6, 9-10, 21, 116, 124, 184, 192, 215, 217-218
assets 235
assign 19
assigned   26, 34, 118, 129, 134-136, 143, 173, 176, 190, 225
assignment   5, 143, 172, 214
assist   67, 162, 207
assistant   8
associated   138, 185, 229
assume   182, 218
Assumption   3, 131
assurance   121, 175, 177, 190, 194, 199, 206
assure 47, 68, 209
attached   154
attainable   32
attempted   29
attempting   73
attendance   28
attendant   67
attended   28
attention   13, 103
attitude   239
attitudes   201
attributes   4, 81, 125, 142, 168, 203
audited   139, 240
auditing   21, 74, 132, 209, 225
auditors   68
audits 244
auspices   9
author 1
authority   123-124, 136, 174, 220, 242-243
authorized   121, 135, 225, 238-240
automatic   239
available   20, 22, 24, 28, 39, 49-50, 102, 108, 140, 146, 153,
168, 181, 183, 185, 188, 197, 206, 217, 221, 230, 243
Average   13, 23, 34, 48, 57, 69, 80, 106, 231
averse 230
avoiding   184
background   11, 209
backing   145
backup   130
backward   204

balance   47
bandwidth   232
barriers 47, 219
Baseline   4, 37, 121, 164
baselined   38
baselines   26, 31
basics 105
Beauty 82
because   40, 45, 156
become   84, 91, 120, 127
becomes   207
before 10, 29, 74, 120, 122, 139, 147, 182
beginning   2, 16, 23, 35, 48, 57, 69, 80, 106
begins 206
behavior   215, 239
Behaviors   41, 207
behaviour   229, 237
behaviours   197
belief   12, 17, 24, 36, 49, 58, 70, 81-82
believable   102
believe82, 95
benefit 1, 18, 66, 71, 221
benefits   22, 50-51, 81, 84, 94-95, 101, 105, 111, 132, 216-217, 241
besides   153
better 8, 28, 38, 43, 154, 163, 188, 206-207, 212, 215, 234
between   39, 47, 55, 127, 151, 153, 159, 166, 194, 199, 219, 226, 235, 238
beyond   215
bidder 238
bidders   238
biggest   38, 67, 160, 222
blinding   50
Blokdyk   9
boards 68
bottleneck   141
bought11
bounce   51, 55
boundaries   31, 121, 214
bounds   31
Breakdown   3-4, 63, 133-134, 150
briefed29
briefly   244

brings 25
broken 56
broker 229
brought   81
budget   63, 71, 102, 118, 121, 135, 152, 154, 161, 182, 225, 229, 231-232, 234
budgeting   135
budgets   101, 135-136, 173, 225, 236
building   18, 74, 110, 150, 227
business   1, 8, 11, 17, 22, 24-25, 30-33, 40, 46-47, 50, 52, 54, 63-64, 76, 79, 84-85, 88, 90-92, 96-97, 102-103, 105, 110, 126, 129, 131, 136, 158, 161, 164, 197, 205, 219, 226, 233, 242
busywork   109
button 11
buy-in 99, 234
buyout 118
calculate   147
calibrated   166
called 236
cannot 147, 157, 161
capability   18, 42
capable   8, 34
capacities   86, 221
capacity   18, 223
capital 101
capture   37, 76, 239
captured   40, 99, 138, 190, 202
capturing   206
career 128, 174
careers   93
carried 197
cascading   44
cash-drain   113
Cashflow   113
categories   223
category   26
caused   1
causes 42, 49, 52-53, 56, 74, 119, 172, 225
causing   19, 194
celebrate   211
central 206
certain 58, 181, 219
chaired   9

challenge   8, 45, 206
challenged   82
challenges   82, 108, 145
Champagne   9
champion   32
champions   170
chance   184, 188
change   6, 17, 33, 54, 63, 67, 75, 86, 89, 96, 112, 119, 123-124, 130, 134, 147, 157-158, 170, 177, 183-185, 187, 194, 196, 202-205, 220-221, 237, 239
changed   33, 91-92, 101, 125, 162, 164, 243
changes   17, 44, 60, 67-68, 74, 79, 82-83, 104, 109, 120-121, 123, 135-136, 150-152, 159, 166, 173, 177, 196-197, 202-205, 217, 238-239
Changing   97, 180
channels   196, 221
chargeable   225
Charter   2, 31-32, 110, 119, 138
charters   29
charting   190
charts 37, 46, 50
cheaper   38, 43
checked   70, 78, 125
checklist   9, 90
checklists   159
choice 26, 89
choose   12, 67
chosen109
circumvent   20
claimed   1
classified   121, 136
cleaning   26
clearly 12, 17, 24, 27-28, 33, 36, 49, 58, 70, 81, 130, 158, 174-175, 215
client   9, 11, 46, 83, 233, 244
clients 26, 186, 221
climate   210
closed 77, 138, 176, 204, 240
closely 11
Close-Out   7, 239, 241
closest 84
Closing7, 51, 235
Closings   38

252

Coaches   26, 34, 170
cognitive   223
colleague   104
colleagues   97, 154
collect 42, 76, 162, 166, 212
collected   24, 28, 39, 46, 50, 55, 59
collection   37-39, 42, 44, 53, 171
college   62
collusion   238
combine   63
coming   52
command   71
commit   216
commitment   82, 170, 196
committed   30, 99, 185, 190-191
Committee   176, 191
common   161, 176
community   155, 162-163, 183
companies   1, 9, 207
company   8, 38, 43, 56, 91, 96-97, 102-104, 154, 168, 206,
231
companys   231-232
comparable   118
compare   54, 63, 228
compared   84, 159, 167
comparing   65, 118
Comparison   12, 192
compatible   204, 224
compelling   30
complaint   208
complaints   208-209
complete   1, 9, 12, 23, 30, 129, 140, 142-143, 151-152, 154-
155, 168, 181, 183, 214, 218, 234, 239
completed   13, 25, 27, 31-32, 122, 129, 147, 155, 164, 212, 239
completely   85
completing   91, 133
completion   26-27, 62, 146-147, 159, 161, 212, 228, 235
complex   8, 46, 95, 227
complexity   41, 45, 203
compliance   52, 131-132, 209, 230
comply   238
components   37, 46, 131
compute   13

computing   85
concept   64, 129, 145, 170
conceptual   199
concerns   19, 47, 84, 178, 231
concrete   215
condition   75
conditions   70, 84, 164, 212
conduct   229
conducted   61, 131, 202, 204, 229, 237
conducting   54
confidence   147
confirm   13
conflict120, 202, 214
conflicts   212, 214
conform   131
connected   156
connecting   89
consensus   214, 241
consider   19-20, 193
considered   19, 22, 44, 229
considers   56
consistent   41, 75, 136, 223, 226, 229
constantly   178
constrain   135
Constraint   3, 131, 229
consultant   8, 161
consulted   98
consulting   39
consults   55
consumers   101
contact   8, 159, 177
contacts   100
contain   22, 77, 119, 215, 223
contained   1
contains   9
content   32, 192, 244
contents   1-2, 9
context   199
continual   11, 76-77
continuity   47
contract   7, 135-136, 147, 152, 160, 193, 201, 225, 237, 239-
240
contracted   195

contractor   7, 124, 129, 135-136, 160, 231
contracts   25, 138, 158, 194, 230-231, 238-240
contribute   209
control 2, 63, 70-71, 73-75, 78-79, 119, 123, 135, 162, 172-173, 191, 202, 206, 226
controlled   51, 135, 238, 242
controls   22, 50, 52, 60, 67, 72, 76-78, 189, 238
convenient   40, 45
convention   102
converge   224
conversion   131
convey   1
cooperate   162
Copyright   1
correct36, 70, 119, 139, 156, 159, 167
correction   136
corrective   74, 152
correctly   209
correspond   9, 11
corruption   237
cosmetic   132
costing45
counsel   192
counting   84, 156
counts 84
course 33, 227
covering   75
covers 229
coworker   83
craziest   89
create 11, 19, 84, 99, 102, 166, 169
created   49-50, 92, 112, 152, 183, 188, 221
creating   8, 38, 194
creativity   66
credible   162
crisis   17
criteria 2, 6, 9, 11, 25-26, 32, 67, 72, 82, 92, 94, 107, 113, 127, 157, 162, 167, 192-193, 209, 239
CRITERION   2, 17, 24, 36, 49, 58, 70, 81
critical 28-29, 32, 38, 50, 72, 75, 87, 90, 109, 131, 135, 141, 144, 191, 193, 207, 215, 235
criticism   49, 216
crucial 52, 172, 198

crystal 13
cultural58
culture 33, 54, 169, 174-175
current31, 36, 39, 47, 50, 54-56, 71, 82, 85, 91, 98, 100, 125, 132, 135, 147, 153, 170, 173, 175, 183-184, 198, 235
currently   34, 206, 217
custom23
customer   11, 21, 25, 28, 30, 32-33, 47, 60, 72, 78, 86-88, 92, 102, 104, 111, 125-126, 164, 184, 186-187, 200, 202, 211, 225, 230, 233
customers   1, 20, 27, 33, 37, 40, 44-45, 47, 51, 54, 84, 86, 90, 96, 99, 103, 105, 120, 144, 166, 180, 184, 188, 225-226
cut-down   227
cutting 186
damage   1, 180
Dashboard   9
dashboards   79
day-to-day   76, 89
deadline   238
deadlines   22, 97, 138, 144
deceitful   83
decide65, 174-175
decided   67, 211
deciding   88
decision   6, 51, 62-64, 66, 109, 182, 206-207, 214
decisions   60, 67, 79-80, 114, 174, 198, 206, 211-212, 235
dedicated   8
deeper   13
deepest   9
defect 42
defective   229
defects   40
define 2, 24, 28, 33, 47, 56, 123, 133, 139, 206, 209, 223
defined   12-13, 17, 22, 24-28, 30-34, 36, 40, 49, 51, 58, 70, 81, 134, 142, 158, 169, 175, 190
defines 19, 29, 32, 151
defining   8, 110, 191
definite   77, 142
definition   139, 158, 164, 176, 184
degree   62, 121, 215-217, 223-224, 238
delays 140, 154, 156
delegated   34, 230
deletions   79

deliver 20, 29, 60, 85, 91, 154, 161, 163, 211
delivered   39, 94, 165, 218, 221, 236, 244
deliveries   237
delivering   217
delivers   150
delivery   21, 84-85, 229, 240-241, 245
demand   104, 187
demands   184, 224
department   8, 102, 201
depend   200
dependent   85, 124
depends   103
deploy 99
deployed   79
deploying   39
derive 72, 145
Describe   22, 61, 120, 127, 129, 144-145, 231-232
described   1, 125, 204
describing   27
deserve   241
deserving   200
design 1, 9, 11, 26, 59, 61, 67, 71, 85-86, 117, 132, 222, 230, 243
designed   8, 11, 51, 59, 61, 69
designing   8
desired24, 60, 150, 205, 227, 241
detail   41, 45, 69, 133, 142, 154
detailed   50, 56, 121, 131, 135
details 197
detect 70, 168
determine   11-12, 82, 93, 97, 140, 152-153, 162, 192, 213, 217,
241
determined   53, 94, 171, 186, 191, 237
determines   160
detracting   87
develop   58, 62, 65, 118, 124, 133-134, 183, 216
developed   9, 11, 25, 28-29, 32, 41, 61, 67, 118, 131, 136, 145,
152, 158, 171, 196, 198, 205, 227
developer   186
developers   202
developing   55, 68, 157, 217
device 209
diagnostic   189
diagram   4, 53, 118, 146-147, 157

diagrams 190
dictates 156
Dictionary 3, 135
differ 198
difference 130, 151, 153, 157, 166, 194, 199, 207
different 8, 28, 31-33, 53, 94, 114, 207, 241
difficult 140, 142-144, 146, 160
difficulty 184
dilemma 103
direct 136, 160, 173, 225, 243
direction 33, 38, 43, 119
directly 1, 51, 54, 109, 114
directors 229
Directory 6, 211
Disagree 12, 17, 24, 36, 49, 58, 70, 81
disaster 47
discarded 82
discovered 64
discovery 221
discuss 213
discussed 229
discussion 47
display 46
displayed 28, 37-38, 40, 55
disputes 214, 239
disqualify 99
disruptive 54
distribute 211
Divided 23, 34, 48, 57, 69, 80, 106
document 11, 25, 119, 125, 130, 167, 206, 212, 244
documented 30, 41, 72-73, 75, 77, 108, 121, 130-131, 139, 175, 196, 226, 233
documents 8, 135, 169, 213, 218
domain 45
domains 103
dormant 100
driving 87, 92
duration 4, 115, 133, 146, 152, 154, 185, 189
durations 29, 156
during 33, 64, 109, 121, 131, 148, 159, 161, 185-188, 206, 241, 243
dynamic 41
dynamics 27

earlier 87, 153
Earned 7, 152, 172, 227-228
economical   82
Economy   68, 114
eDiscovery   206
edition 9
editorial   1
educate   243
education   21, 77, 209
educators   114
effect 44, 183, 191, 235
effective   17, 93, 95, 97, 101, 132, 155, 189, 207-210, 218,
243-245
effects 41, 135, 144, 183
efficiency   53, 77, 153
efficient   139, 200
effort   40, 44, 68, 98, 118, 120, 124, 135-137, 221
efforts 29, 122
electronic   1, 238
element   136, 139
elements   11-12, 72, 93-94, 129, 138, 198, 225-226
Elevator   126
eliminate   188
embarking   30
embeddings   168
emergent   41
emerging   21, 78, 217
emphasis   207
employed   158
employee   66, 101, 231
employees   51, 83, 96, 103-104, 208, 218, 238
employers   112
empower   8
enable 54
enablers   94
encourage   66, 79
endemic   208
engage   91, 214, 216, 224
engagement 37, 112, 179, 213
enhance   73, 75, 153
enhanced   93
enough   8, 89, 96, 103, 109, 127, 176, 181

ensure 29, 32, 67, 93, 95, 98-99, 104, 113, 115, 121, 166, 170, 175, 192, 194, 212, 215, 221, 230
ensured   238
ensures   99
ensuring   10, 98, 210, 227
entered   129
Enterprise   200
entire   135, 186
entities 46, 118
entity   1
equipment   21, 166, 209
equipped   28
equitably   34
equivalent   191
errors   98, 132, 136, 229-230
escalated   109
essence   111
essential   68
Essentials   89
establish   58, 162, 186
estimate   43-45, 110, 118, 161, 192, 234
-estimate   159
estimated   26-27, 44, 99, 163, 182, 192, 231-232
estimates   4, 25, 48, 53, 118, 121, 131, 138, 152, 159-160, 164, 190, 225
Estimating   4, 138, 154, 159, 162
estimation   65, 158
ethical 96, 221, 233
ethnic   102
evaluate   65-66, 139
evaluated   108, 193, 209
evaluating   67
evaluation   68, 72, 168, 192-193, 216, 221, 224
evaluative   199
evaluators   219
events 44, 66, 110, 152-153
everyday   52
everyone   29, 34, 168, 170, 229
everything   206
evidence   13, 39, 168, 183, 200, 237-238
evolution   36, 243
evolve 79
exactly175

example   2, 9, 14, 21, 53, 79, 119, 121, 136, 139
examples   8-9, 11, 110
exceed   133, 146
exceeding   37
excellence   8
excellent   38
except 136
exception   218
excess 135
exclude   60
execute   109
executed   37-38, 205
Executing   6, 131, 187, 198
execution   109, 119, 198
executive   8, 102, 110, 139, 190
executives   90
Exercise   146
exerted   242
existing 11-12, 40, 45, 79, 83, 110, 198, 218, 237
exists   147
expect 118, 161, 241
expected   22, 29, 98, 105, 109, 116, 119, 153, 159, 161, 206,
225
expend   40
expensive   46, 140
experience   84-85, 95, 154, 174, 186, 193, 209, 225, 231
experiment   92
Expert 9
expertise   63, 118, 160, 176, 214, 229
Experts 26, 172
expiration   147
explain 244
explained   11
explicitly   90
explore   53
extension   237
extent 12, 28, 69, 115, 135, 159, 243
external   29, 87, 138, 168, 186, 195, 237
facilitate   12, 21, 79
facilities   192, 210
facing 20, 103
fact-based   216
factors 44-45, 62, 87, 109, 162, 199

failed   45
failing   94, 182
failure   47, 100, 114, 131, 153, 209
fairly   34
familiar9
fashion 1, 26
favorable   172
feasible   43, 56, 100, 162, 203
feature10
features   233
feedback   2, 11, 25, 33, 45, 108, 174
figure   42
finalized   14
financial   38, 50, 53, 55, 91, 115, 136, 145, 180, 182
fingertips   10
finish   140, 145, 227-228
finished   121, 145
fitness   230
flying   26
focused   41
focuses   109
follow   11, 73, 93, 99, 152, 234
followed   31, 121, 159, 180
following   9, 12, 170, 229
follow-up   115, 161
for--and   72
forecast   227
forefront   90
foresee   145
forever 101
forget   10
formal 7, 95, 124, 131-132, 184, 202, 209, 223-224, 233-234
formally   34, 109, 135, 152-153, 157, 165, 190
format 11, 211
formed30, 34
formula   13, 86
Formulate   24
forward   92-93
forwarded   226
foster   81, 104, 183
framework   71, 101, 171
freaky 96
frequency   25, 74, 171

frequent   139, 191
frequently   45-46, 113
friend   103-104
friends 215
frontiers   63
full-blown   39
full-scale   67
fulltime 191
function   113, 129, 161, 190
functional   136
functions   31, 53, 83, 86, 126, 175, 190, 224
funded236
funding   89, 104, 108, 124, 131, 221, 236
further 172, 182-183
future   8, 41, 46, 71, 135, 159, 183, 187, 225
gained 51, 72, 78, 217
gallons 139
gather 12, 36, 88
Gathering   126
General   142, 234
generally   200
generate   51-52, 64
generated   56, 59, 108
generation   9
geographic   214
Gerardus   9
getting 165, 207
glamor 26
global   68, 85
governance   83, 175, 217
governing   179
graded   203
graphs 9, 37
gratitude   9
greater   119
greatest   121
ground 45, 50
grouped   142
groups 94, 120-121, 132, 151, 201
growth 50, 87, 144
guaranteed   33
guidance   1
guidelines   207, 237

guides 119
hampered   243
handle 120, 148, 187
handled   193
handling   184, 208
happen   21, 182, 188-189
happening   85
happens   8, 11, 89, 97, 101, 126, 161, 163, 182, 188-189, 239
hardest   44
hardly 228
hardware   198, 243
having 182, 209, 214, 226
hazards   188-189
health 208
healthy   189
hearing   102
helpful 36
helping   8, 116
higher 136
high-level   31-32, 110
highlight   175, 183
high-tech   91
hijacking   97
hinder 132
hiring   62, 79
Historical   162, 225
history 141, 165, 243
hitters 50
hitting 227
holders 120
honest 96
humans   8
hypotheses   49
identified   1, 19, 25, 32-33, 39-41, 44, 46, 51, 55-56, 120-121,
129, 139, 153, 159, 166, 175-176, 183, 188, 191, 194, 207, 211,
213, 219, 225-226, 244
identify 12, 21-22, 46-48, 53-54, 113, 144, 162, 172-173, 178
ignoring   90
imbedded   72
immediate   45
impact 5, 29, 33, 38, 40, 42-45, 47-48, 59, 95, 116, 125, 160, 182-
184, 186, 194, 204, 217, 219-220, 236
impacted   132, 242

impacts   113, 132, 154, 180, 202, 241
Implement   18, 40, 70, 172
implicit 101
importance   193, 224
important   21, 45, 51, 54, 62, 82-83, 90, 96, 100, 114, 116,
198, 215, 217, 222
improve   2, 11-12, 56, 58-61, 63-65, 67-68, 111, 160, 168,
173, 212, 217, 222, 243
improved   59, 61-62, 69, 78, 236
improves   108
improving   62, 201
incentives   79
incident   206
include   60, 64, 113, 129, 135-136, 153, 192-193, 195, 209
included   2, 9, 126, 162, 187, 231-232, 240
includes   10, 39
including   18, 26, 29, 31, 38-39, 53, 63, 68, 72, 74, 76, 131,
208, 219, 225
inclusion   208
increase   69, 96, 153
increasing   83, 207
indemnity   229
in-depth   12
indicate   46, 75, 94, 99
indicated   74
indicators   43, 47, 51, 54, 74, 115, 180, 226
indirect   136, 160, 172
indirectly   1
individual   1, 39, 120, 140, 174, 214-215, 224, 231, 241
inducting   209
industry   84, 92, 103, 144
infected   189
infection   189
infinite 85
influence   63, 112-114, 178, 207, 220, 242
influences   213
informal   224
informed   86, 108, 120
ingrained   77
inhibit 58
in-house   110
initial   88
initially 135

265

initiated   163, 204
Initiating   2, 104, 108
Initiation   243
initiative   12, 170-171, 179
Innovate   58
innovation   51, 53, 68, 72, 85-86, 104
innovative   84, 115, 154, 163, 222
inputs   27-28, 50, 74
insight 49, 51
insights 9
inspired   100
Instead100
instructed   123
insurance   229
insure   93
insurers 68
integrate   76, 91, 118
integrated   108, 192
integrity   102, 204
intended   1, 63-64
INTENT 17, 24, 36, 49, 58, 70, 81
intention   1
interact   86
interest 153, 188, 201
interests   46, 48, 114, 178
interfaces   131
interim 97
internal   1, 29, 87, 89, 109, 144, 168, 226
interpret   12-13
intervals   139, 190
interview   101
introduce   41
introduced   26, 217, 221
intuition   43
invaluable   2, 9, 11
investment   21, 166, 170, 187
investors   68
invited 237
invoices   139
involve 100, 114, 196
involved   20, 53, 68, 104, 116, 132, 138, 174, 178, 184, 191,
195, 201, 221, 230, 240, 242
involves   73, 123

involving   209
isolate 42, 172
issues   64, 109, 114, 125, 129, 131, 139, 146, 148, 166, 211, 213, 219, 226, 241
iteration   190
iterative   126
itself   1, 20
jointly 215, 223
journey87
judgment   1
kicked 81
killer   84
knock-on   183
knowledge   11, 29, 37, 51, 63, 71-72, 75, 77-79, 81, 84, 95, 105, 135, 153, 164, 174, 196, 214, 217, 239
labeling   209
lacked 92
largely 56
latest 9
leader 17, 32, 51, 54
leaders29, 34, 55, 81, 99, 166, 190
leadership   30, 33, 68, 99, 130
learned   7, 71, 76, 99, 170, 235, 241, 243
learning   71-72, 75, 207-209, 217
length 189
lesson 235, 243-244
Lessons7, 67, 76, 99, 170, 241, 243-244
levels   18, 25, 50, 54, 71, 92, 113, 134, 170, 189, 226
leverage   31, 68, 76, 84, 163, 213
leveraged   29
leveraging   217
liability 1, 229
licensed   1
lifeblood   105
lifecycle   40
lifecycles   64
Lifetime   10
likelihood   59, 63, 159, 182, 184, 187, 194
likely   71, 104, 114, 187, 206
limited 11
linear 126
Linked 25, 206
listed   1, 177

listen   93
liters   139
locally 237
location   196, 206, 213
logged177
logical 148, 225
longer 71
longest152
long-term   79, 83, 98
losses   41
magnitude   62
maintain   70, 87, 102
maintained   135, 173
majority   214
makers 74, 109
making   17, 51, 60, 63-64, 81, 116, 171, 182, 214, 237
manage   48, 56, 60, 84-85, 109, 111, 114, 124, 127-128, 139,
143, 157, 170, 186, 211, 220
manageable 34
managed   8, 31, 129, 177, 233
Management 1, 3-6, 11-12, 18-19, 21, 26, 31, 34, 37-38, 55, 60,
63, 68-69, 79, 84, 89, 96, 116, 118-120, 123, 129-131, 138, 142,
151-153, 157-159, 161, 165-166, 170, 172-173, 176, 178, 180, 185-
186, 190, 192-194, 196, 199-200, 214, 221, 225, 228, 239, 241, 244
manager   8, 12, 20, 27, 32, 105, 109-110, 186, 191, 201, 233,
243
managers   2, 107, 119, 199
manages   111, 231
managing   2, 10, 107, 112, 123, 184, 194, 220, 241
mandatory   204, 242
manner   132, 139, 173, 198, 202, 226, 233, 235
mantle 103
mapped   33
margin 226
marked   129
market 40, 144, 180, 227
marketable   180
marketer   8
marketing   89, 101, 166
material   110, 172, 192
materials   1, 194, 213
matrices   127
Matrix 3, 5, 113, 127, 172, 186

matter 26, 47, 216
mattered   244
maximize   209, 217
maximizing   94
meaningful   37, 89, 136, 215, 223, 226
measurable   30, 32
measure   2, 12, 20-21, 30-31, 36-44, 46-47, 52-53, 58, 60-61,
65-66, 73, 75, 77, 110, 115, 162, 169
measured   21, 36-37, 39-42, 46-47, 60, 70, 74, 136, 167, 188
measures   38-39, 41-43, 45-48, 50, 53-54, 74-75, 115, 222
measuring   135, 209, 226
mechanical   1
mechanism   184, 203, 241
mediated   214
medium   216, 227
meeting   27, 45, 78, 175, 178, 194, 200, 207, 209-211, 214,
230
meetings   27-29, 33, 207
megatrends   105
member   6, 30, 88, 150, 200, 213, 217, 223
members   25-26, 30, 33-34, 130, 138, 174, 179, 191-192, 195,
212, 214-216, 219, 223-224
membership   215
memorable   168, 215, 223
messages   213
method   26, 38, 92, 143, 155, 158, 169, 214, 216
methods   25, 33, 43, 120, 158, 162, 166, 185, 194, 213
metrics 5, 32, 42, 79, 139, 168-169, 190, 196
milestone   4, 110, 138-139, 144
milestones   31, 112
minimize   116, 180, 236
minimizing   94
minimum   34, 232
minutes   27, 66, 211
missed 45, 102
Missing 98, 142
mission 55-56, 96-97, 100, 174, 224
Mitigate   116
mitigation   156, 159
Modeling   56, 170
models 49, 94, 103, 114
modified   69
modify 218

moments   52
momentum   100, 102
monetary   18
monitor   64, 73, 75, 78-79, 120, 162
monitored   73, 120, 154
monitoring   7, 72-73, 76, 120, 123, 148, 157, 173, 180-181, 190, 194, 221
monthly   226
months66, 110, 155, 218
motivation   73, 76
moving   93
multiple   123, 158, 181, 219
mutual 116
myself 97
narrative   166
narrow 55
national   198
nature 41
nearest   13
nearly 95
necessary   42, 49, 56, 66, 75, 83-84, 103, 117, 162, 173, 205, 209, 216, 221, 238, 243
needed   18, 21, 23, 28, 50, 68, 72, 74, 76, 115, 162, 167, 176, 178, 238, 241
negatively   153, 182, 198, 242
negotiate   83
negotiated   103
neither 1
network   4, 146-147, 157, 220, 223
networks   198
Neutral12, 17, 24, 36, 49, 58, 70, 81
nonlinear   168
normal 77, 189, 199, 237
notice 1, 115
noticing   207
notified   197, 239
notify   214
number   23, 34, 38, 48, 57, 69, 80, 88, 106, 142, 151, 184, 187, 246
numerous   239
objective   8, 40, 206
objectives   17, 21, 24-25, 30, 55-56, 72, 76, 90-91, 94, 97, 114-115, 132, 153, 158, 164, 176, 182, 189, 194, 200, 211, 229, 244

obligates   152
observed   59
obsolete   105
obstacles   20, 154, 163
obtain 234, 241
obtained   25, 47
obvious   89
obviously   13
occurring   58
occurs 18, 74, 187, 235
offerings   54, 63
office   200, 239
officers 229
officials 240
onboarding   159
one-time   8
ongoing   46, 60, 74, 154, 230
on-going   120
online 11
on-site 212
operate   214
operates   103
operating   6, 75, 165, 202, 213, 221
operation   78, 155
operations   12, 73, 76-77, 79, 164-165, 209
operators   73
opponent   206
opponents   113, 178
opposite   82, 103
opposition   83
optimal   65-66, 193, 232
Optimize   63, 73
optimized   101
option 89
options 20, 183
organized   142, 238
organizm   189
orient   78
oriented   159
original 22, 206, 238
Originate   74, 178
others 108-109, 156, 162, 164-165, 168, 172, 178-180, 186, 191,
203, 207, 216, 223, 230, 242-243

otherwise   1, 58
outcome   13, 150
outcomes   41-42, 61-62, 73, 100, 113, 115, 154, 163, 227, 229-230, 241
outlined   73
output 31, 44, 70, 75
outputs   27, 50, 74, 115, 148, 195
outside 66, 89, 213
Outsource   240
overall 12-13, 21, 76, 92, 146, 156, 193, 195, 198, 206, 222, 231, 235, 237
overcome   154, 163
overhead   136, 226
overheads   177
overlook   219
overlooked   190, 235
oversees   108
oversight   129, 176, 230
overtime   148
owners 134
ownership   33, 77, 116
package   135
packages   135-136
packaging   209
paragraph   104
parallel   146
parameters   75
paramount   184
Pareto 50, 190
partial 237
particular   36, 53
Parties 211, 239-240
partners   20, 99, 103, 221, 242
pattern   142
paycheck   96
paying 103
payment   138-139, 239
payments   238
pending   204
people 8, 19, 38, 49, 65, 68, 79-80, 84, 86-87, 93, 97-98, 100-101, 109, 131, 172, 178, 181, 183-184, 187, 194, 196, 200, 209, 227
perceived   216
percent   86, 97

percentage   127
perception   61, 68, 96, 168
perform   19, 26, 34, 124, 132, 141, 185, 188, 202, 215
performed   60, 121, 127, 140-141, 160, 173, 181, 192, 209, 212
performing   136, 173, 182, 193, 218
perhaps   227
period 59, 161, 172
periods 136
permission   1
permit 41
person 1
personally   128
personnel   18, 73, 147, 157, 170-171, 176, 208-209
pertinent   73
phases 40, 109, 236
picked 92
places 160
planet 79-80
planned   37-38, 73, 77-78, 108, 135, 140, 229, 241
planners   74
planning   3, 9, 71, 79, 115, 117-118, 121, 131, 135-136, 146,
148, 150, 158, 201, 208, 243
Planning-   74
platforms   218
Pocket 155
Pockets   155
points   23, 34, 48, 57, 69, 80, 106, 144, 171
policies   92, 118, 175
policy   30, 74, 148, 237
political   58, 93, 144, 178, 220, 243
population   115
portfolio   96
portray 50
position   175
positioned   162
positive   67, 102, 119, 132, 210
positively   182, 242
possible   37, 45, 52, 55, 59, 64, 70, 85, 89, 209, 216, 237
potential   19, 34, 44, 47, 58, 65, 67, 99, 101, 105, 113, 159,
182, 194, 219, 221, 226
practical   56, 58, 64, 70, 200-201
practice   41, 114
practiced   108

practices   1, 11, 76, 79, 158, 217-218, 233
precaution   1
precede   147
predict73, 202
Predictive   150
predictor   151
predictors   203
preferred   241
pre-filled   9
prepare   152, 174, 179, 214
preparing   156, 241
present   46, 71, 138, 199, 215
presented   211
preserve   28
pressure   237
pressures   144
prevalent   196
prevent   41, 165
prevents   17
previous   29, 109, 157, 231
previously   121, 204
prices   192
primary   124, 150
principles   116
printing   9
priorities   43, 46, 164
prioritize   173
priority 224
privacy   169, 230
probable   186
problem   17, 19-20, 24, 28-29, 31-32, 51, 56, 187, 200, 206,
216, 225, 228
problems   19-20, 22-23, 42, 58, 62, 65, 74, 104, 125
procedure   152, 214
procedures   11, 73, 75, 77, 121, 131, 135, 148, 166, 191, 206,
209, 214, 226, 230
Process   1-15, 17-23, 25-35, 37-42, 44-57, 59-116, 118-127,
129-135, 138-148, 150-168, 170-178, 180-188, 190-192, 194-196,
198-206, 208-209, 211-215, 217-219, 221-223, 225-231, 233-245
processed   238
processes   33, 41, 47, 53-56, 72, 79, 108-109, 170, 194-197,
205, 208, 214, 233
procuring   135

produce   109, 148, 161, 195, 201
produced   67
produces   143
producing   127
product   1, 11, 44, 51, 54, 84, 105, 110, 129, 144-145, 165,
168, 180, 194, 198, 201, 205, 212, 219, 227, 229, 233, 236, 244-245
production   60, 214
products   1, 19, 21, 38, 99, 127, 136, 153, 194, 199-200, 205
Profession   180
profile 183, 208
Profitably   73
program   17, 62, 108, 119, 161, 166, 220, 243
programme   114-115, 117, 198, 221-222
programs   68, 118, 200, 202, 229
progress   29, 36, 66, 76, 81, 83, 110, 116, 162, 171, 199
prohibited   136
project 2-4, 7-9, 19, 22-23, 25, 38-39, 53, 55, 72-73, 77, 83, 85, 88,
93, 95-96, 99-100, 104-105, 107-116, 118-121, 123-125, 127, 129-
134, 138-147, 150-163, 165, 168, 172-173, 175-177, 182-187, 190-
191, 194-195, 198-201, 204-205, 211, 219, 221-223, 225, 227-228,
231, 233-236, 240-245
projected   173, 226
projects   2, 82, 86, 107, 114-116, 118, 127, 129-130, 133,
153, 174, 181, 185, 187, 199-200, 211, 218, 227-228
promising   84
promote   38, 49, 152
promptly   109
proofing   59
proper 138
properly   11, 24, 29, 44, 108, 135-136, 237-238
proponents   178
proposals   74, 192
proposed   18, 45, 61, 121, 124-125, 192, 196, 231-232
Propriety   221
protect   52, 105
protection   94, 180
proved 233
proven 194
provide   18, 49, 93, 100, 112-113, 137, 147, 154, 163, 169,
216, 224-225
provided   9, 13, 71, 121, 190, 193
provider   229
Providers   113

provides   150
providing   112, 164
public 229
publisher   1
pulled 86
purchase   9, 11, 238
purchased   11
purchases   237
purpose   2, 11, 97, 111, 114, 129, 150, 162, 194, 207, 215, 223
pursued   82
pushing   96
qualified   34, 176
quality 1, 5-6, 11, 36, 41-42, 52, 55, 74, 109, 115, 120-121, 129, 160, 166, 168-170, 175, 177, 190-191, 194, 199, 206, 208-210, 212, 229-230
quantities   192
quantity   238
quarterly   225
question   12-13, 17, 24, 36, 49, 58, 70, 81, 92, 181, 220
questions   8-9, 12, 56, 154, 178, 199, 220
quickly 12, 51, 54-55
radically   54
raised 139
Raters 218
rather 41, 86
rating 193, 203
ratings 192
rational   226
rationale   207
reaching   97
reactivate   100
readings   78
realised   194
realistic   118, 199, 223
reality 164
realized   95, 233
really 8, 19, 172
reason 82, 90
reasonable   104, 118, 120, 138, 237
reasons   30, 177
rebuild 84
receive   9-10, 27, 39, 196

received	29, 105, 158, 208, 216, 244
recently	11, 102
recipient	239
recognised	230
recognize	2, 17-18, 22, 69, 153
recognized	19, 23, 62, 217
recognizes	20
recommend	103-104, 179
recorded	176
recording	1, 214
records	20, 50, 135, 167, 173, 225, 240
recovery	47, 131, 156
redefine	26
re-design	56
reduce194	
reduced	189
reducing	78, 83
references	246
reflect	51, 135-136, 241
reform	46, 74, 100
reforms18, 43, 45	
regarding	98, 201
Register	3, 5, 112, 182-183, 187
regret	64
regular29, 232	
regularly	25, 28, 33
regulated	202
regulation	238
reinforced	221
reject	123
rejecting	152
rejection	209
relate	199, 205
related39, 41, 77, 108, 164, 175, 203, 228	
relation	19, 97
relations	71, 87, 183
relative76, 224	
relatively	95
release190	
releases	231
relevant	11, 32, 46, 49, 71, 84, 105, 115, 174, 197, 226
reliable28	
relocation	118

relying 215
remaining 156, 163
remains 121
remedial 41
remedies 45
Remember 155
remove 64, 188
remunerate 65
renewed 153
repeat 109
repeatable 229
rephrased 11
replace 110, 235
report 6-7, 42, 78, 169, 200, 208, 211, 223, 231, 241
reported 168, 172, 219, 228
reporting 76, 121, 123
reports 39, 112, 119, 158, 226
repository 176
represent 60, 205
reproduced 1
reputation 91, 105
request 6, 56, 124, 164, 202-205
requested 1, 60, 109, 192-193, 204
requests 177, 202-203, 238
require 39, 79, 135, 148
required 21, 30-32, 62, 68, 109, 124, 126, 140, 142, 146, 154, 174, 177-178, 182, 196-197, 230, 242
requiring 112, 239
research 84, 214, 217
resemble 199
reserved 1
reserves 173
reside 176
Resistance 196
Resolution 49, 214
resolve 212
resolved 109, 139, 214
Resource 4-5, 9, 113, 121, 131, 139, 143, 148, 150, 176, 180, 201
resources 2, 9, 22, 24, 28, 47, 63, 68, 72, 78, 85, 87, 92, 98, 108-109, 113, 118, 126, 138, 140, 142-143, 146-147, 157, 163, 190, 195, 220, 242
respect 1

respected   238
respond   115
responded   13
responding   183
response   17-18, 72, 74, 77, 79, 231
responses   182
responsive   155, 162
result   51, 60, 67, 161, 163, 196, 204, 215, 237, 239, 241
resulted   75
resulting   50, 119, 129
results 9, 29, 41, 54, 58-59, 61-63, 69, 71, 74, 109, 116, 119, 121,
142, 157, 161-162, 199, 221, 233, 244
retain 81, 105
retrospect   86
return 42, 67, 166, 170
returned   26
revenue   38, 43
review 11-12, 164, 166, 177, 202, 206, 208, 214, 217, 243
reviewed   28, 139, 157, 169, 190, 209, 244
reviewers   216
reviews 11, 121, 131, 138, 184, 230
revised 53, 75, 189
revisions   239
revisit   207
reward 38-39, 53, 200
rewards   79
rights   1
routine 70, 136, 226
rushing 178
safely   230
safety 99, 213, 230
samples   166
sampling   166-167, 190
satisfied   98, 123, 233, 243-244
satisfies 227
satisfy   108
satisfying   91
savings 25, 53
scenario   199
scenarios   202
schedule   3-4, 34, 38, 63, 71, 89, 118, 124, 138, 146, 156-157,
172, 177, 180, 182-183, 192, 204, 211, 226, 231
schedules   147, 182

scheduling   135, 158, 173
scheme   77
Science   155
Scientific   155
Scorecard   2, 13-15
scorecards   79
Scores 15
scoring 11
screen 213
screening   118, 168, 230
seamless   93
second   13
section 13, 23, 34, 48, 57, 69, 80, 106
sector 227
Secure 87
Securing   37, 98
security   21, 72, 112, 131, 168, 204, 230, 241
segmented   32
segments   33, 94
select 54, 76
selected   61, 65, 162, 185, 226
selecting   92, 118, 214
Selection   6, 192
seller   152, 160
sellers 1
selling 89, 144, 207, 225
-selling 226
senior 96, 99, 166
separated   137
sequence   140
sequencing   100, 176
series   12
service 1-2, 8-9, 11, 44, 61, 68, 84, 92, 105, 144-145, 165, 180, 201,
244
services   1, 9, 38-39, 93, 98, 194, 208, 210, 221, 231-232,
234, 237-239
session 136
setbacks   51, 55
several 9
severely   56
Severity   182
shared 78, 115, 162
sharing 75, 213

should 8, 22, 31-32, 39-40, 54, 59, 61, 64, 67, 69, 77, 85, 92-93, 95, 101, 110, 112, 116, 119, 132, 135-136, 142, 154, 158, 160-161, 174-175, 180, 184, 187-188, 192-193, 202, 204, 211, 218, 225, 236-237, 241
-should 165
Sigmas 109
signature   95
signatures   148
signed 129
signers 240
similar 25, 29, 50, 54, 63, 120, 141-142, 165, 168
simple 95, 173, 227
simply 9, 11
single   104, 161
single-use   8
situation   21, 36, 225, 227
skeptical   101
skills   18, 40, 42, 45, 81-82, 105, 153, 174, 183, 199, 216-217, 223, 230
slippage   184
smallest   20, 66
social 89, 101, 210, 243
software   21, 108, 115, 121, 132, 180, 185, 190, 198-199, 202, 231, 243
solicit   33
soluiton   232
solution   43, 49, 56, 58-59, 61, 63-67, 70, 130, 232
solutions   39-40, 45, 58-59, 61, 64-65, 67, 118
solving 216
Someone   8
something   95, 135, 209
Sometimes   39
sought 114
source 6, 104, 192, 208
sources   50, 53, 64, 88, 186
special 9, 71, 110
specific   9, 19, 21, 30, 32, 93, 124, 140, 142-144, 146, 148, 160, 175, 185, 201, 205, 237
specified   97, 236, 244
specify 209
Speech   126
spoken 102
sponsor   21, 118, 233, 241

sponsored   32
sponsors   20, 171
stability 47
staffed 24
staffing 18, 79, 121, 131, 191
standard   8, 108, 148, 231-232
standards   1, 11-12, 77, 94, 131-132, 167-168, 170, 194, 205,
230
started 9, 145, 147
starting 12
startup 102, 110
start-up   113
stated 90, 92
statement   3, 12, 62, 65, 96, 129, 160-161, 194
statements   13, 23, 31-32, 34, 48, 51, 57, 69, 80, 106, 153
status 6-7, 49-50, 108, 121, 123, 139, 158, 173, 190, 200, 211,
226-228, 231
Steering   139, 176, 190-191
stopper   125
stored 123
strategic   71, 76, 90, 158
-Strategic   79
strategies   83, 115, 130, 156, 159, 207
strategy   22, 67-68, 74, 87-88, 92, 117, 206, 229
strengths   233
strong 174
stronger   96
Strongly   12, 17, 24, 36, 49, 58, 70, 81, 203
structure   3-4, 63, 83, 95, 133-134, 150, 193, 223
structures   117, 136
stubborn   83
stupid 86
subject 9-10, 26
submission   237
submit 11, 237
submitted   11, 204
submitting   169
subset 20
sub-teams   216
succeed   103
success   18, 20, 30, 36, 42, 44, 46-47, 59-60, 70, 84, 86-87,
94, 97, 100, 105, 114, 153, 160, 184, 196, 198, 200, 206, 222, 235
successful   50, 67, 78, 85, 88-89, 102, 151, 179, 198, 200